GARDENS OF JAPAN

JAPANESE ART

Peonies in Spring, chart on page 80.

Susan Witt's
Classics for Needlepoint

Oxmoor House, Inc. Birmingham

Classics for Needlepoint

Senior Editor: Candace N. Conard
Editor: Jo Voce
Design: Carol Middleton
Cover photograph: Mac Jameison
Photography: Mac Jameison, John O'Hagan,
    Mike Clemmer, and Charles Walton
Illustrations: Steve Logan, Don Smith

Special thanks to Frances Sterne, Jewel Callaway, Sally Foley, Tanny Cunningham,
Helen Jordan, Nancy Smith, Frances Blanchard, and Mary Bryant.

Library of Congress Catalog Number: 80-84410
ISBN: 0-8487-0525-4
Manufactured in the United States of America
First Printing 1981

Table of Contents

Introduction

Twenty years ago in an art class at Stephens College in Columbia, Missouri, I looked at my art work, compared it to all of my classmates' projects, and decided I would be better off in another major. My dream world was turned around in a hurry. The competition and my reaction to it were so staggering that I decided to become an accountant instead of a dress designer. I went from the excitement of high fashion to the drudgery of putting little numbers inside little boxes—the antithesis of creativity.

The little boxes, as you can see, no longer hold numbers. Instead, they contain the symbols of my designs, and these are the outlet for my creativity.

The accounting background came in handy when I started my own needlepoint business seven years ago. Mine was not the usual type of needlepoint business; I started with nothing but yarn, canvas, needles, and the few books of charts that were available back then. I did not carry a single kit. I taught classes of decorative stitches, bargello, making charts—anything to keep people from buying prestitched canvas and filling in the background or from working on painted canvases.

The artists who paint canvases consider needlepoint canvas to be like artist's canvas—a flat surface—and they paint as though a person doing the needlepoint could see what is in the holes. There are also the canvases carried over from "coloring book" days that have all areas outlined in gray or black lines. Those gray or black lines are not supposed to be worked with gray or black yarn, but what color they should be is anybody's guess.

With such strong feelings about painted and preworked canvases, I focused my needlepoint business on charted designs. However, I found that there are some people who cannot or will not work from a chart, so I devised my own method of transferring the designs to canvas. After you work one piece by my technique, I know you will never look at another commercially painted canvas. You will be able to recognize the quality of design and workmanship that can be obtained only through my method of counting and marking. To my knowledge, no canvases on the market, other than the canvases I have sold, are marked with the technique used in this book.

Needlepoint as an art can never be realized until designs of quality are executed correctly. I have included the charts for my teaching pillows not so much to teach you a particular design as to begin a process of working with your hands. The more dexterity you have, the more accurately and comfortably you can place your stitches on the canvas. There are hints with each of the designs and hints throughout the Portfolio of Stitches. Among these you are sure to find techniques to make your work more professional looking. The method of counting and marking plus the stitch information should prepare you for the best work possible.

Most of my basic designs are taken from classic artifacts such as plates, screens, or rugs. There is only one piece that is a direct copy; Peonies in Spring is taken from an antique dish. The other motifs were created from scattered bits of design combined to make my own interpretations. I see beautiful objects and, when I begin to work, the motifs come back to me in different forms. In one piece, I may use an idea that I originally saw in a piece of china and another from a rug, but my design will be different from either.

My hope is that my designs will inspire you to improve your needlepoint skills and to begin designing your own motifs based on the things that surround your own life.

Selecting Supplies

As a needleworker, shop owner, and teacher, I am convinced that all of your needlepoint supplies should be the best you can find. Needlepoint involves an investment of your time and concentration, and your supplies should be worthy of your efforts. The supplies recommended here are the ones that I use for my own needlepoint and that I recommend to the people who come into my shop.

CHOOSING A SHOP

All supplies should fall under the heading of choosing a shop and shop owner. The owner and the people who work in the shop are as important as the quality of the materials they sell. Ask if the shop owner offers assistance or advice with a purchase of supplies. Most shops teach lessons and charge for this. The formality and regularity of the lessons are fine, but you still need a shop owner who can answer questions when you get into trouble.

You should also be able to turn to the shop owner for advice about finishing a piece of needlepoint. Shops should be able either to finish the piece on the premises or to recommend an upholsterer or other finisher. There are many secrets in correctly finishing needlework, and for this reason, it is important to remember that people who do it for a living do it every day and you do not. I would never finish a piece of needlepoint myself just to save money. After working the needlepoint design with the best materials, I want the finishing to be done by an experienced professional.

Check the references of a finisher and check his prices to be sure you are getting what you want for all the effort you have already put into the project. Ask questions. Will he finish a pillow or chair seat without cutting into the needlepoint? If you can look inside a pillow and find that the canvas has been cut to the sewing line, run, do not walk out of the shop. You cannot remove the backing of the pillow to replace it without ripping into the needlepoint. When you arrange to have chair seats put on, demand that the canvas not be cut away from the worked area, and, needless to say, do not allow anyone to cut into the worked area. When you spill food on a seat and take it off for cleaning, you cannot get it back on the chair if the canvas has been cut. The best guide to finishing your needlework is to put as much effort into finding reliable people to finish a piece as you have put into the other facets of the project.

CANVAS

Since the canvas is the foundation for needlepoint, it is essential that you buy the best.

There are two types of canvas. Mono is the kind used in the designs for this book. Mono canvas has single vertical and horizontal threads and is used for most purposes. Penelope, the other type of canvas, is woven with two closely spaced vertical and horizontal threads; this canvas is usually used for designs with petit point because the threads can be split to work very small stitches on the same canvas with larger stitches. Mono canvas is more frequently used today.

The size of mesh (intersections of horizontal and vertical threads) of a canvas is indicated by a number. A #10 canvas will have ten vertical and ten horizontal intersections in one square inch. A #13 canvas will have thirteen vertical and thirteen horizontal intersections to the square inch. A higher number of mesh count indicates a higher number of threads to the inch and, subsequently, more stitches needed to cover the threads.

Canvas is available in two colors, brown and white. Brown canvas is a good choice for designs with multiple stitches or bargello because the canvas will be less noticeable between stitches. White canvas is generally used for any designs worked predominantly with basketweave and continental. It is used for designs that are marked with the count and mark technique described in the next chapter.

All the designs in this book can be worked on #13 mono canvas. (One design, Museum, is worked on #10 but could work just as well on #13.) I have found that #13 is a size in which the mesh is not large enough to be coarse nor

(Continued on page 9.)

Opposite: Patterned Iris, chart on page 44.

Opposite: Iris Companion, chart on page 46.

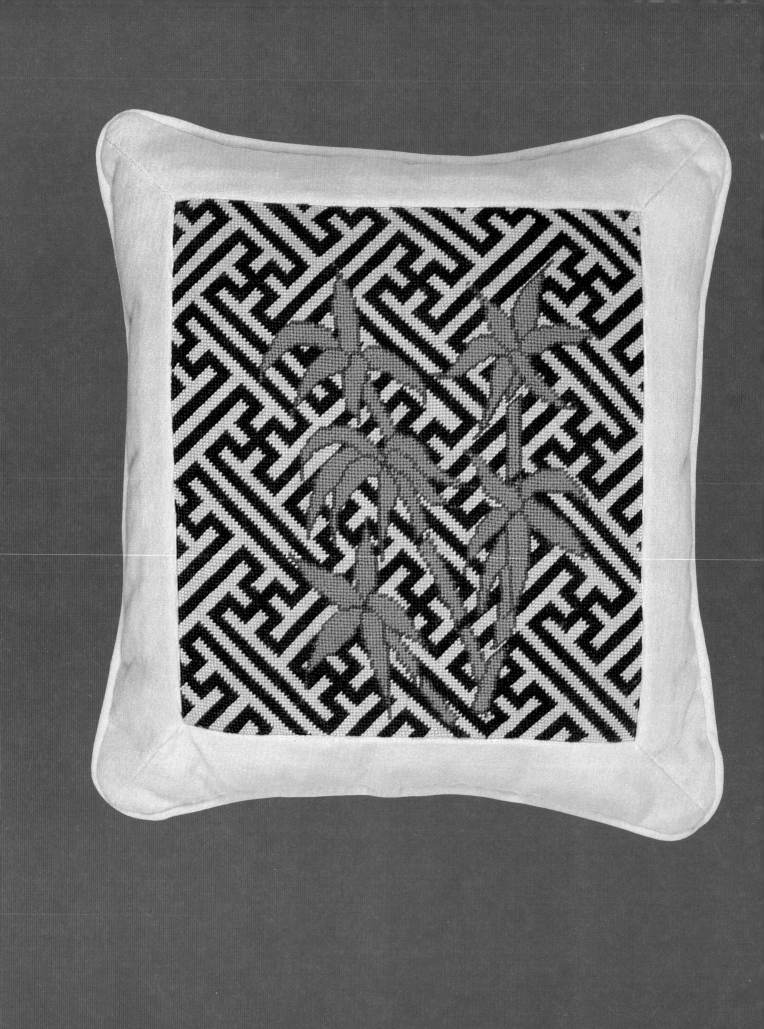

small enough to be blinding to work. It is the best size for bargello worked with 3-ply yarn.

When I use white canvas, I use Zweigart canvas. It comes in all standard meshes and is consistently of good quality. When I use brown canvas, I use Elsa Williams's brand. These brands are usually available through shops, but you may also contact the companies at the addresses given in the list of Suppliers, page 121.

There are other canvases on the market—and some good ones. My personal preferences are based simply on what I have found to be best for me and on what I have seen other shops buy in the wholesale market.

Changing Meshes of Canvas

Any design can be put on any size of mesh of canvas, although there are some designs that look better on small mesh and others that look better on larger mesh. If a design is simple and has very little shading or detail, the smaller canvas mesh will work better. If a design is detailed and has lots of shading, it can be put on any size. All designs look better on smaller canvas, but you would not want to waste time doing a circus elephant on #18 canvas for a child's room when it would be just as effective on #10. Canvas size is a personal choice. The designs in this book are accompanied by canvas mesh sizes, but feel free to use another size if you prefer. Just remember that if you use a smaller mesh (larger number), the finished size of the needlework will be smaller; a larger mesh (smaller number) than that recommended will result in a finished piece that is larger.

If you use a different mesh of canvas from that recommended with the chart, you must refigure how much canvas you will need. To do this, take the chart thread count (indicating the number of boxes on the chart and the number of stitches on the pillow) and divide by the number of the canvas mesh. For example: if your chart thread count is 175 × 151 and you want to use #10 canvas, divide each dimension

by 10. You will need a piece of canvas 17½″ × 15″ for the design itself. Add 2″ in each margin for blocking and finishing. This makes a 21½″ × 19″ piece of canvas. The figures in the book are given in half inches. Anything below a half inch is dropped to the lower number, and anything over a half inch is raised to a higher number.

Preparing Your Canvas

The instructions that accompany each chart include the canvas mesh size (in most cases #13 canvas), the color (white or brown), and the dimensions for the piece of canvas needed for the design. If you change mesh sizes, the canvas size will change. The sizes given with the charts will indicate if an allowance for a bargello border is included. All the sizes also include 2″ of extra canvas on each side of the design for seams or other finishing requirements.

After cutting your canvas to the required size, bind the edges with masking tape or sew around the edges with a sewing machine to prevent ravelling.

YARN AND NEEDLES

All of the colors in the charted designs have Paterna® yarn (Paternayan Brothers) numbers listed with the color codes. This yarn is widely available in shops, or to contact the company, see the list of Suppliers, page 121. Paterna® yarn is all 3-ply persian yarn. It comes in a wide assortment of colors and shades of colors.

Persian yarn, because of its three plies, can easily be adapted to any size of canvas and any stitch. It is excellent for using 3-ply with #10 canvas and for splitting to 2-ply for #13 canvas. Different stitches require different plies to cover the canvas adequately. The average ply requirements are given with each of the stitches described in the Portfolio of Stitches, page 21. Specific ply instructions also accompany each design.

Some shops sell yarn by the string. The large skeins of yarn are cut into strings that are 33″ long and sold singly, so you can purchase only a small amount. If you are using a chart that

Opposite: Bamboo, chart on page 64.

has only a small amount of one color, it would be to your advantage to find a shop that sells yarn by the string.

Dye lots present a problem with any yarn. A variation of the shade that is hardly noticeable when the yarn is in your hand suddenly becomes a glaring difference in tone when it is used across half the background. To avoid such color shifts, always buy all the yarn of one color that you will need to complete the project. You will have to rely on the shop owner to help you determine the correct amount of yarn. I have not given the yarn requirements on any of the designs because beginners and people who work on a frame use more yarn than an experienced non-frame worker will use. Always buy extra yarn for the background color; no shop can guarantee having the same dye lot over even a short period of time.

Never use a length of yarn in your needle that takes more than one natural pull to bring it through the canvas. If you are using two pulling motions for a stitch, your yarn is too long, and you will wear out the yarn before you finish the length. If the yarn has become fuzzy when you have finished working it, the yarn is too long. Try a shorter length for easier and better coverage of the canvas.

The needles used for needlepoint are called tapestry needles. These have a blunt point and a large eye. The needles are sized according to the size of the eye—the larger the eye, the smaller the number. I use a #20 needle on #13 canvas and a #18 needle on #10 canvas. Buy a package with several sizes so that you can pick the one that you like best.

Moisture in your hands can cause the needle to become tarnished or rough. If this occurs, run the needle in and out of a sand or emery bag (these are usually attached to pin cushions). If this does not clean the needle, throw it away.

Threading the Needle
Sometimes trying to thread the ends of heavy yarns through the slender eye of a needle can be an exasperating chore. There are two tricks you can use, however, to easily overcome this obstacle.

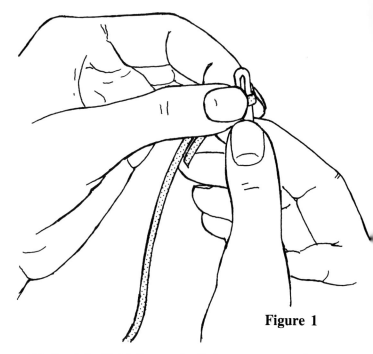

Figure 1

Method 1. Fold the end of the yarn over the needle. Pinch the fold tightly between your thumb and index finger. (Figure 1.) Slide the needle out and push the eye over the folded yarn, using a sawing motion to help it slide over the yarn. (Figure 2.) Then pull the yarn through with your fingers until you have disengaged the looped end.

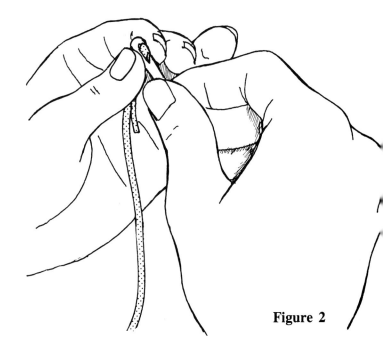

Figure 2

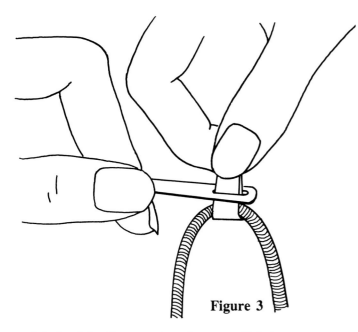

Figure 3

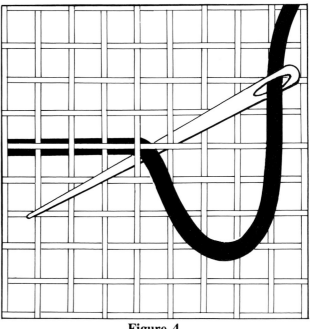

Figure 4

Method 2. Cut a strip of paper slightly narrower in width than the size of the needle eye. Fold the paper in half and slip the yarn end into the fold. Insert the narrow cut ends of the paper strip into the needle eye, and then pull the paper and yarn through the eye. (Figure 3.)

Beginning and Ending Strands of Yarn

The yarn used in needlepoint should be anchored on the back of the canvas but not tied in a knot. The following method can be used to start the first strand or to begin new strands once the work is in progress. Bring the yarn up from the back of the canvas in the first hole of your stitch pattern, leaving an end about 1″ long on the wrong side of the canvas. Point this end in the direction in which you will be stitching and hold it flat against the canvas with one hand. Then work your stitches over the yarn end, fastening it securely against the back of the canvas. (Figure 4.)

To end a strand, weave the yarn through the yarn on the back of the canvas. When only 2″ or 3″ of the strand you are working with remain, or when you need to end one color and begin another, bring the needle through to the wrong side of the work and weave the yarn for about 1″ through the backs of the adjacent stitches. Then trim the excess yarn close to the canvas. Avoid weaving dark colored yarns through light ones whenever possible.

After you have finished the first strand, try to stagger the beginnings and endings of subsequent pieces so that they do not fall at the same spot on each row. When beginning or ending with the basketweave stitch, always come in horizontally on an "uphill" row and vertically on a "downhill" row. If you begin or end on the diagonal line, you will create a thick place that makes a line on the front.

MARKING PENS AND PAINT

Pens and paint are used to transfer a design from a chart onto the canvas. I recommend two types—Nepo® and AD Markers. (See Suppliers, page 121.) Both of these pens come with a fine point, and both are waterproof. If you prefer to use another brand of pen, always test to be sure the ink is waterproof. You will need several colors on some charts.

Even though these pens are waterproof, it is a good idea to spray the canvas with a clear fixative to be sure that colors will not run.

Gesso or white acrylic paint is needed for covering mistakes you may make with the pens. These will cover most errors for a short length of time. When you are handling the canvas in the course of working, the paint will sometimes flake off.

MISCELLANEOUS SUPPLIES

You will need scissors for cutting the canvas to size and for cutting the yarn. You may wish to work with a thimble. A small emery bag is handy for cleaning needles. A needle threader strong enough to pull yarn—not just sewing thread—through the eye of the needle is an alternative to the threading methods diagrammed in this book.

The use of a frame is a matter of personal preference. Many people prefer to work with the canvas in their hands. Others like to work with a canvas mounted on a frame. Frames reduce the portability of needlepoint, but they do keep the needlepoint from pulling out of shape. Work with whatever makes you comfortable.

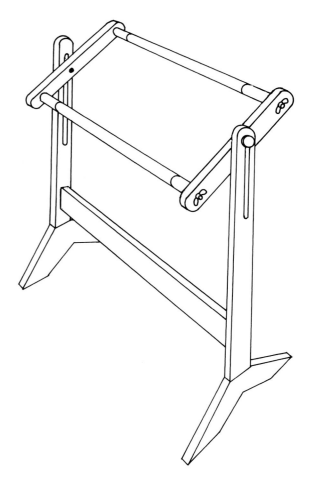

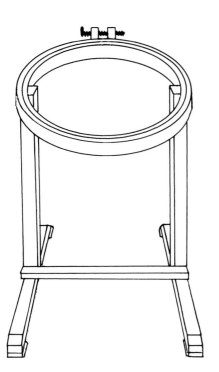

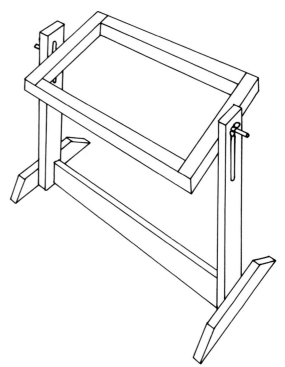

Working with the Charted Designs

Y ou can work any of my designs featured in *Classics for Needlepoint*. With a chart, I can show you where I placed every stitch, and when you follow the charts, your design will be exactly like mine. Such accurate reproduction of design is the great advantage of my count and mark technique.

TYPES OF CHARTS

There are two types of charts in needlepoint: box charts and line charts. Each of my charts is labelled by type.

In box charts, boxes represent intersections (crossings of vertical and horizontal threads) on the canvas. *The "hole" in the chart is not the "hole" in the canvas.* The square that holds the symbol is the crossing of the threads (or the intersection) of the canvas. The stitch is made *across* this intersection in the color indicated on the chart. The symbols (x, o, /, etc.) represent the colors given in the color code accompanying each chart. Box charts are used to indicate color and, although continental and basketweave are expected because they are used more often than other stitches, the stitch is not usually shown on a box chart. To determine the kind of stitch, it is necessary to refer to the instructions that accompany the charts.

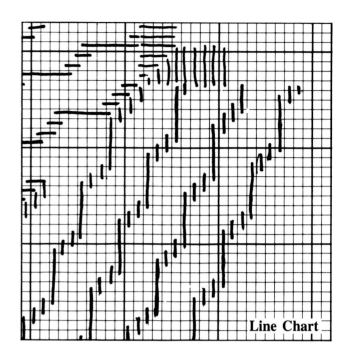

Line Chart

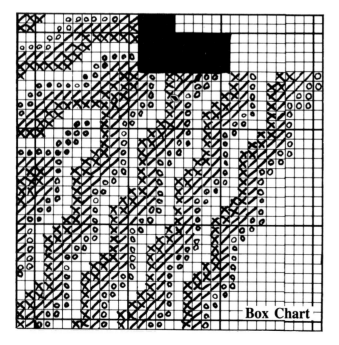

Box Chart

On a line chart, horizontal and vertical grid lines represent horizontal and vertical lines on the canvas. These charts show the stitches—not the colors. When you make the stitch on the canvas, your chart and canvas should look the same. To determine colors to use with these charts, it is necessary to refer to the accompanying instructions or to the box charts for the same area. Line charts—for decorative stitches and bargello—must be counted; do not mark the canvas.

Since line charts show the length and direction of stitches and box charts show color, it is sometimes necessary to use both charts in order to present a design completely. There is no way to show the decorative stitches and bargello on a line chart that requires a number of colors. With the bargello borders, both types of charts are given—line charts for the pattern and box charts for color combinations. To combine the charts, work the stitches shown on the line charts with yarn in the colors shown on the box charts.

COUNT AND MARK TECHNIQUE

Working from charted designs has usually been a matter of finding the center of chart and canvas and starting to stitch. With a ruler or pair of scissors, you kept your place on the chart and tried to work the canvas. I know a better and more enjoyable way to work from a charted design.

I find the center of my canvas, and using pens in the required colors, I put a dot on the intersections of the canvas that correspond with the boxes on the chart. When I have finished marking, I have a canvas that shows every stitch of the entire design. I can then relax and work the design, concentrating on my stitch tension. I never lose my place; I can pick up and move my needlework at my convenience. An area of basketweave can be worked smoothly because the design is on the canvas rather than on the chart.

All designs with box charts can be marked with my technique; line charts are never marked on your canvas.

To transfer the designs, first have these materials handy: canvas, chart, waterproof pens for marking, white acrylic or gesso paint, and a fixative. Then follow the count and mark technique outlined below. I recommend working the small sample at the end of this chapter as a practice piece for learning to use my count and mark method.

Prepare Your Canvas

Refer to the instructions that accompany each chart for the canvas size for that project. Be sure you are using the size mesh indicated in the canvas size given with the design or figure a new canvas size as explained on page 9. Canvas sizes given with each project allow for 2″ margins for finishing. If there is an allowance for a border around a central design area, that will be included in the canvas size.

Cut the canvas to size. Bind the edges with masking tape or stitch around the edges with a sewing machine.

Find the Center of Your Canvas and Chart

Find the center of your canvas by folding it into quarters. (The center is the best place to begin marking for most of the designs; instructions that accompany a few charts may suggest a different point to begin for that design only.) Fold directly along threads of your canvas so that the center falls on top of an intersection of a horizontal and vertical thread. This is indicated by the black threads in the diagram.

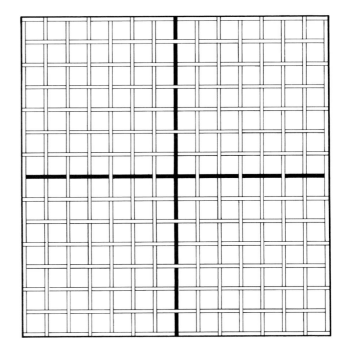

Find the center of the chart by finding the intersection of the horizontal and vertical rows that are marked *center* on the chart.

Mark Your Canvas

Take a pen in the color indicated for the center stitch on the chart and "dot" the intersection. Continue to mark each intersection as indicated on the chart with a pen in the color that matches the color symbol. From the center, mark outward by the quadrants formed when you folded the canvas, marking first the upper right quadrant, then the lower right, and continuing with the lower left and upper left quadrants. This is shown in the photograph on the following page.

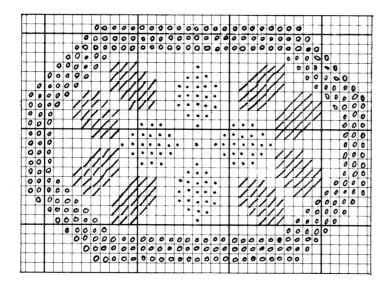
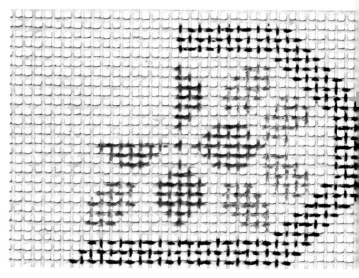

Work outward in relation to the parts already marked; do not try to jump around from one area to another.

When the design changes colors, change pens. Do not try to mark all the blue, then all the green. If you make a mistake, correct it immediately with the white acrylic or gesso paint. A mistake in one place will throw something else out of position, so correct mistakes as you go.

Often you will not have pens that are the colors indicated by the color code. Use the pens you have, but you may want to make your own color code on a card to remind yourself of the color of pen you used and the color of yarn you want it to represent. Try not to use a very dark color of pen to represent a light color of yarn. Yellow yarn may not cover black pen marks.

Avoid making any unnecessary division marks on the canvas. Do not try to mark off grid lines because they are too difficult to cover, particularly with a cream background.

As you practice this technique, you will develop a "touch" for placing the marks, and marking will become easier.

Transfer the sample design to scrap canvas as many times as it takes to build your confidence.

After drawing it, work the sample and you will see that it is easier to work over a marked canvas such as this than over any painted piece you have ever bought.

Once your entire design is marked on the canvas, you are ready to begin the fun—stitching.

Practice

Canvas Size: Scrap of any mesh

Color Code:
- ⊡ dark blue
- ⊡ dark red
- ⧄ green
- ☐ cream for background

Stitches: continental and basketweave

Instructions:

Find the center of your canvas as described on page 15.

Beginning with the center of the design, mark your canvas as explained on page 15.

Mark the top of the canvas so you remember to work basketweave without turning the canvas. Work the design in continental and basketweave (2-ply yarn), using continental for outlines and single rows of stitches and basketweave for larger areas.

Fill in the background in basketweave with cream.

Opposite: Lattice & Flowers, chart on page 48.

Lattice & Tulips, chart on page 50.

Lattice & Lace, chart on page 52.

Portfolio
of
Stitches

The Portfolio of Stitches illustrates all the stitches used in my designs. The diagrams for each of the stitches are to be used in basically the same way. Following the numbered steps, always come up with the needle from the back of the canvas on odd numbers (1, 3, 5) and go down through the canvas from the top of the canvas on the even numbers (2, 4, 6).

Each strand of persian yarn can be divided into three plies, and different stitches require different plies to cover the canvas. The best rule for checking the ply necessary is simply to see if the canvas is covered. If you can see canvas between stitches, you are either working with the wrong ply of yarn or your tension is too tight. Try increasing the ply if the canvas is not covered. Yarn ply is indicated for each stitch as it is used on the canvas meshes in my designs.

Some stitches in this portfolio have specific tension instruction. If you pull the stitch too tightly, the finished piece of needlework will be impossible to block. Any time you see the canvas pulling out of position, you are pulling your stitches too tightly. Tension should be a natural, rhythmical motion. You can try my little trick to help. When you first sit down to work, work where you have a small area of design or color (never background). If you take out all the day's frustrations on the little areas, you will soon calm down enough to work the background smoothly.

Check the stitch diagrams and instructions for the direction of the stitch on the canvas. Basketweave, for example, *must* be worked without changing directions, but four-way bargello can be done only by working from the four sides of the canvas. In some designs, the major portion is worked in basketweave but surrounded by a four-way bargello border.

It is a good idea to practice new stitches on a scrap of canvas before trying the stitches within a design. Different stitches require a different tension, a different ply of yarn, a different direction. Here in the Portfolio of Stitches, you are given the basic "how-to" of the stitches along with my suggestions for how to make each stitch easier and better.

BASIC STITCHES

The basic stitches of needlepoint are continental and basketweave. Both stitches slant from lower left to upper right across one intersection of canvas and look alike on the top of the canvas. Continental, however, should be used only as an outline stitch, whereas basketweave is always used to fill in large areas of design.

BASKETWEAVE STITCH

This is the most important stitch in needlepoint. After you have learned to follow the basic diagrams, continue practicing and studying to perfect the stitch.

Working with the weave of the canvas is important in doing basketweave correctly. Look closely at a piece of mono canvas. It is a woven material with intersections of two threads crossing each other. A vertical intersection is one in which the thread of canvas on the top of the intersection runs in a vertical direction. When the thread on top of the intersection runs in a horizontal direction, this is a horizontal intersection.

Now look at each diagonal line across the canvas. Each diagonal line is made up of intersections that are consistently horizontal or vertical. Basketweave, which is worked on a diagonal line, should be worked in a pattern consistent with the direction of the weave of the canvas. A diagonal line in which all the intersections are vertical should be worked as a "downhill" row. A diagonal line with all horizontal intersections should be worked as an "uphill" row.

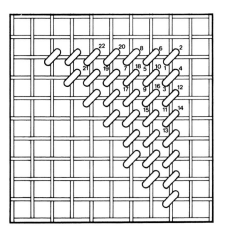

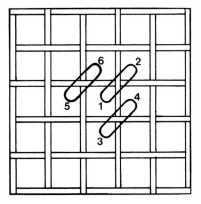

To set up a background of basketweave, follow the numerical sequence in the diagram. If the first stitch—or first row—of your background is over a vertical intersection, it represents a "downhill" row. The second row would then be over horizontal intersections and be worked "uphill." If the first intersection on your background is horizontal, it would represent an "uphill" row and the next row would be a "downhill" row.

Lines or ridges on the front of basketweave may be caused by several things, but the most common cause is making two "uphill" or two "downhill" rows together. This breaks the weave on the back of the canvas and causes a line on the front.

Try to remember that vertical is "downhill" and horizontal is "uphill." If you learn to think this way, you will never have the problem of not knowing where you stopped last time you were working. You will not even have to check the back of your canvas; everything is right in front of you. Following the weave of the canvas also makes the yarn move easily into the holes on the canvas, thus giving a much smoother look to your work.

If you have difficulty mastering the basketweave stitch, go to a shop owner and ask for help. Once you develop confidence and rhythm, you will be working beautiful basketweave with both pleasure and ease.

Binding off or starting a new piece of yarn in basketweave should also be related to the weave of the canvas. If you bind off or start a new piece of yarn by hooking into the diagonal line, you will have a thick place that causes a line on the front of your needlework. When binding off or hooking in, always come in horizontally on an "uphill" row and vertically on a "downhill" row.

Never turn your canvas. Basketweave must be worked in only one direction. You may want to mark the top of the canvas to remind yourself not to turn it.

"Squaring-off" areas will cause lines on the surface of the needlepoint. I have noticed that some people start the background in a corner just as should be done, work a while, and then decide to "square-off" and finish a small square of the background. This does not work well because it divides the canvas into small patches instead of the smooth, continuous area produced by working the diagonal line until an edge of the design is reached. In "squaring-off," the canvas is not uniformly covered on the back, and if the weaving on the back is broken, a line will show on the front. You should stop the diagonal line in the background only on the edge or when your line runs into a patterned area.

Avoid "gouging" the needle into the stitch already in the hole. Gouging splits the yarn and pulls the other stitch too tightly, making it too little. If you are not sure whether or not you are doing this, look at the back of your work and see if all the little "weaves" on your basketweave are the same size. If some rows look smaller than others, you need to practice slipping your needle into the hole without poking the thread already there.

The only time you cannot use basketweave is when you do not have as many as two rows together or more than three stitches of a color in a small area. In these instances, use the continental stitch.

Yarn Requirements: Use 2-ply yarn on #13 canvas and use 3-ply yarn on #10 canvas.

CONTINENTAL STITCH

Note that the diagram for continental has rows in which the numbers appear in different directions. Work a first row of continental with numbers on the diagram pointing in the normal direction. Then turn the canvas to work the second row.

Continental is an outline stitch and should be used very little because too much of it pulls the canvas out of shape and makes the needlepoint look uneven. In large areas, the stitches are never uniform. Use continental for working single rows of a color within a design and as the outline of a design area that is then filled with basketweave.
Yarn Requirements: Use 2-ply yarn on #13 canvas.

DECORATIVE STITCHES

These stitches add texture and interest to the surface of a piece of needlepoint. They may be used in conjunction with continental and basketweave in varying arrangements of color and texture. Interesting in themselves, they may also be combined into designs of only one color.

BACK STITCH

This stitch is used to make a neat finish between rows of straight gobelin. Note how the stitch can turn a corner as neatly as does the straight gobelin with a mitered corner. Yarn Requirements: Use 1-ply yarn between rows of straight gobelin on #13 canvas.

BRICK STITCH

In most of my designs that incorporate the brick stitch, it covers 2 threads of canvas, but it can cover 4 threads or be used in combinations of lengths of stitch.

The brick stitch is a "wrapping" stitch. If you are making the stitch from bottom to top, you cannot change direction and make it from top to bottom without distorting the canvas. In other words, if you do steps 1 and 2, and then shift to 4 before 3 at the top of the stitch, you are not wrapping the canvas and the canvas will

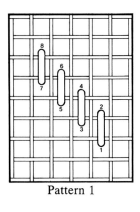

Pattern 1

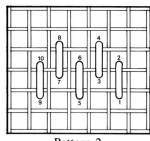

Pattern 2

show between the stitches. A wrapped canvas as shown in the diagram will not leave canvas showing.

Yarn Requirements: Use 2-ply yarn on #13 canvas when covering 2 threads of canvas as indicated in these diagrams. Use 3-ply yarn on #13 canvas when covering 4 threads of canvas.

CROSSED CORNERS STITCH

When repeating this stitch in a border, you may prefer to work all of the large crosses first (steps 1 through 4), then return and do all of the smaller crossings last (steps 5 through 12). Practice to be sure you are comfortable working this stitch before using it in an actual design; a mistake can throw off an entire border.

Yarn Requirements: Use 2-ply yarn on #13 canvas.

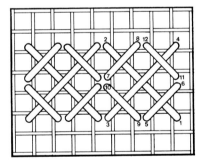

DIAGONAL MOSAIC STITCH

This stitch is worked diagonally across the canvas and works up quickly. It is good for covering large areas.

Do not pull your stitches too tightly, or you will leave holes in the canvas when it is blocked. This stitch can really distort a canvas; practice to avoid the distortion.

Yarn Requirements: Use 2-ply yarn on #13 canvas.

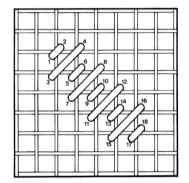

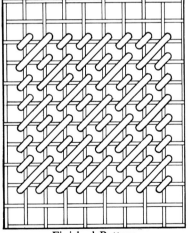

Finished Pattern

DIAMOND CROSS STITCH

This stitch requires more yarn than do many of the other decorative stitches.

Follow the number sequence exactly; it is easy to interchange the last two steps. In working a row or covering a large area with this stitch, all of the stitches must have the final layer of yarn (steps 7 and 8) running in the same direction or the pattern will be interrupted.

In background or other large areas, these stitches are often worked in staggered rows.

Yarn Requirements: Use 2-ply yarn on #13 canvas.

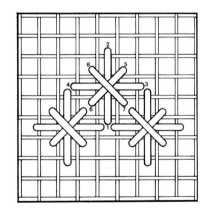

DIAMOND EYELET STITCH

Each even-numbered step of this stitch goes underneath the canvas through a single hole in the center of the stitch. Do not pull too tightly.

In this large stitch, the individual steps are long and somewhat loose, and it is easy to snag or pull out the stitch. Secure the end of the yarn on the back when finished (even a knot is permissible here) so the yarn does not pull out.

Practice on a scrap piece of canvas before working the diamond eyelet in a design; it can be difficult to balance working with the many directions of the stitch and maintaining the correct tension.

Yarn Requirements: Use 2-ply yarn on #13 canvas.

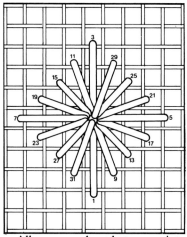

All even-numbered steps go into center hole of canvas.

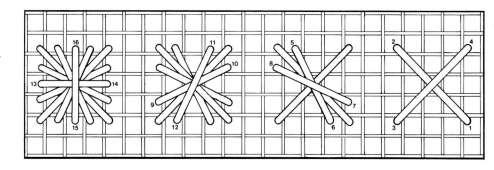

DOUBLE LEVIATHAN STITCH

It is a common error to interchange the last two steps of this stitch. Always be sure the final layer of yarn (steps 15 and 16) is worked vertically.

Yarn Requirements: Use 2-ply yarn on #13 canvas.

LARGE CROSS/STRAIGHT CROSS STITCH

This stitch is composed of two distinct stitches—the large cross (steps 1 through 4) and a smaller straight cross (steps 5 through 8) that fills in between the larger crosses. You can work as numbered on the diagram or first work all of the large crosses in a row or border and then go back and fill in the smaller crosses.

Yarn Requirements: Use 3-ply yarn on #13 canvas.

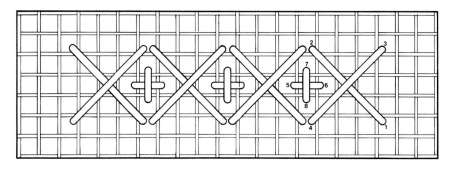

LEAF STITCH

Both the large leaf and the small leaf stitches are used in several of my designs; check the instructions with each design carefully and choose the large or small stitch to match the design requirements.

Begin both the large and small leaf with a stitch at the top of the leaf. Next, work from the top down the left side. Then work from the top down the right side.

To make the small leaf and the large leaf longer, simply extend the sides.

Watch both stitch patterns for the symbol "O." This marks a hole in the canvas that is *not* to be used. It must remain empty to make the stitch work correctly.

If a center line or "stem" down the middle of the stitch is desired, add a line that begins in the hole marked "O" and ends in the last center hole used by the side stitches (marked 11 on the small leaf or 15 on the large leaf).

Yarn Requirements: Use 2-ply yarn on #13 canvas.

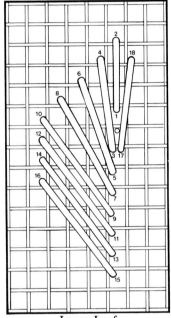

Large Leaf

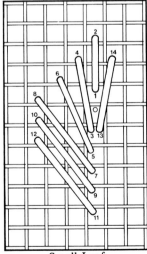

Small Leaf

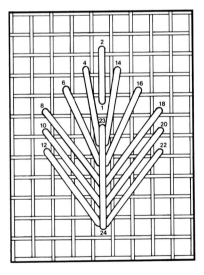

RHODES STITCH

In this large stitch, the individual steps are long and somewhat loose, and it is easy to snag or pull out the stitch. When you have finished the stitch, anchor the thread on the back (even a knot is permissible here) so that you are sure the stitch will not pull out.

Do not pull this stitch too tightly or it will distort the canvas.

Yarn Requirements: Use 2-ply yarn on #13 canvas.

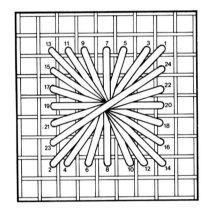

SCOTCH STITCH

Always work steps 1 through 28; then start again with step 1. If you work the first section of stitches (steps 1 to 14) and start over with step 1, it may be hard to block your canvas.

Work steps 1 through 28 all around your project and then return to the beginning of a border to work a second row. Yarn Requirements: Use 2-ply yarn on #13 canvas.

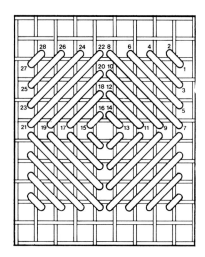

SMYRNA CROSS STITCH

Work so the final layer of yarn (steps 7 and 8) is vertical. Yarn Requirements: Use 2-ply yarn on #13 canvas.

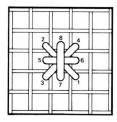

SHELL STITCH

Steps 11 through 14 can be done as you work the larger "crosses," or they can be done as a separate row of stitches after you have finished a row of the larger pattern formed by steps 1 through 10.

In a row of shell stitches, notice that the sides of the stitches share a hole in the canvas. Step 8 of a first stitch and step 2 of the next stitch go into the same hole; step 7 of the first stitch and step 1 of the next stitch go into the same hole.
Yarn Requirements: Use 2-ply yarn on #13 canvas.

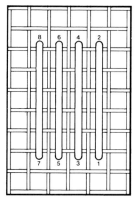

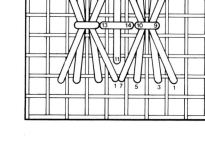

STRAIGHT GOBELIN STITCH WITH A MITERED CORNER

Always work the straight gobelin stitch with a wrapping motion as shown in the diagram. Trying to work from step 8 to step 10 instead of step 9 will distort the canvas, making it show between the stitches.

Work from empty holes (steps 7, 9, 11) into filled holes (steps 8, 10, 12) so that the needle is placed into the filled hole from the *top* of the canvas. If the stitch is reversed, fuzz is dragged from the yarn in the worked area.

Although the straight gobelin must be worked from filled holes when it is between a worked design area and a border, it is still better to work it last.
Yarn Requirements: Use 3-ply yarn on #13 canvas.

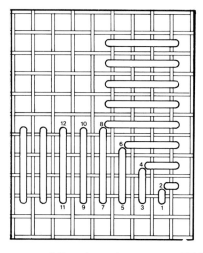

(Continued on page 37.)

Opposite: Imari, chart on page 40.

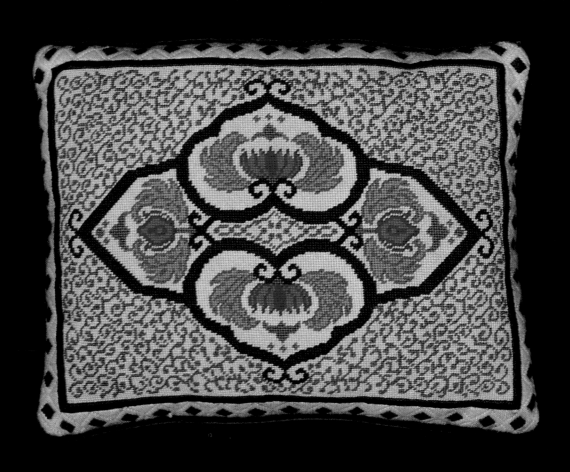

Above: Lotus Blossom,
chart on page 78.

Right: Chinese Symbol for Success,
chart on page 66.

Opposite: Chinese Fertility Symbol,
chart on page 86.

Above: Foo Lion, chart on page 88.

Opposite: Kaleidoscope, chart on page 97.

Above: Oriental Flower, chart on page 42.

Right: Blue Shells, chart on page 92.

TRIANGULAR RAY STITCH

Before working this stitch on a piece of needlework, practice on a scrap of canvas to determine the many directions of the stitch and the correct tension. Do not pull this stitch too tightly.

In this large stitch, the individual steps are long and somewhat loose, and it is easy to snag or pull out the stitch. To prevent the stitch from pulling out, secure the end of the yarn on the back (even a knot is permissible here) when the stitch is finished.

All even numbers (indicating the yarn going from the front of the canvas to the back) are in the center hole of the stitch. Yarn Requirements: Use 2-ply yarn on #13 canvas.

All even-numbered steps go into the center hole.

COMPENSATING STITCHES

Where stitches use more than one intersection of canvas or where two design areas meet, there may be blank spaces around the edges of design areas. These blanks must be filled with less than a whole stitch. Turn to the diagram for the stitch you would work if you had the space. See which portion of the stitch matches the empty canvas, and work that portion. If the portion of the stitch is particularly complicated or if a portion of a stitch must be repeated several times, it is a good idea to practice the compensating stitch on a scrap of canvas.

BARGELLO TECHNIQUES

Most people develop their own way of doing bargello. Some prefer to work from the center of the design out to the edges. Others prefer to begin in the bottom right corner and work to the bottom left corner. Either approach works well. For the best results, find a way to work the design with the needle coming up through the canvas in an empty hole and going down into a filled hole. The reverse movement will fray the yarn.

When it is subjected to hard wear, bargello will not last as long as other types of needlepoint. Enjoy bargello pillows as color accents that you do not subject to much wear.

Brown canvas is the best choice for bargello because it will not be as noticeable between the stitches. Do not pull the stitches so tightly that the canvas shows through.

Always work bargello with 3-ply yarn to cover the canvas. Any time you can see the canvas between stitches, you are either pulling too tightly or not using enough yarn.

BARGELLO

Bargello consists of straight stitches worked in a geometric pattern. These stitches can vary in length and can cover from 2 threads to 6 threads of canvas.

Bargello is a "wrapping" stitch. Follow the numbered sequence to wrap the canvas. If you try to turn the stitch (working 1-2, then 4-3 instead

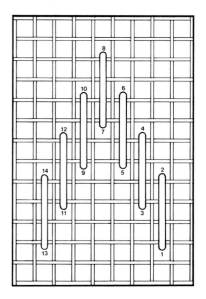

of 3-4), the canvas will be distorted and will show between the stitches.

In this book, line charts indicate the length of the stitches and box charts indicate the colors to be used. Both types of charts may be used to complete a bargello design. To combine the charts, work the stitches shown on the line charts with yarn in the colors shown on the box charts. Refer to the instructions for Working with the Charted Designs, page 13.
Yarn Requirements: Use 3-ply yarn on #13 canvas.

FOUR-WAY BARGELLO

This is simply a straight bargello pattern worked from four different directions and mitered at the corners. In this book, stitches are drawn on the charts, but the charts will be easier to follow if you understand how the stitches work together.

A design in four-way bargello is set up by first finding the center of the canvas and then dividing the canvas into fourths using a simple running stitch along the diagonal lines. The pattern of the stitches, which varies from one bargello design to another, is then applied to each of the four sections between diagonal lines.

Look at the bottom section of the stitch diagram. The stitches are straight and vertical. Turn the diagram so another section is at the bottom.

These stitches are also straight and vertical. Along the diagonal lines established by dividing the canvas, the straight stitches meet in a common hole of canvas. It is this mitering of the straight designs that creates the characteristic appearance of four-way bargello.

A center section of a four-way design is shown. The bargello borders are, of course, bands of bargello that would appear as a frame around the center of the design. The mitered corner stitches are worked into a diagonal drawn from the corner of the worked design to the outside corners of canvas.
Yarn Requirements: Use 3-ply yarn on #13 canvas.

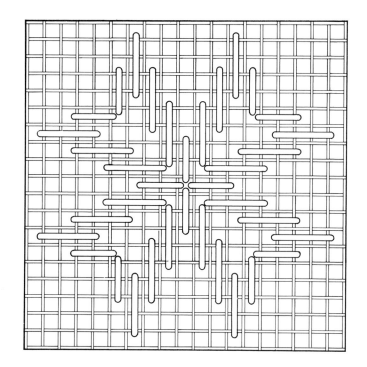

Basically
Basketweave

Basketweave is the workhorse of needlepoint. In the designs in this section, the surface of the finished piece displays the characteristic flat look that we associate with "needlepoint."

The advantages of my count and mark technique, explained on page 15, are most evident in this group of designs. Only by marking your canvas first are you able to work the basketweave smoothly—and stitch tension is so important to the overall appearance of your needlework.

Read carefully the instructions that accompany the charts for the individual designs; special hints will help you to complete the designs.

IMARI

In the resplendent colors of traditional Imari ware, this design that is featured on the cover of *Classics for Needlepoint* combines complexity and order. Do not be intimidated by the many patterns. Taken one at a time, each of the elements can be readily transferred to canvas with the count and mark technique.

Notice as you work with the design that it is composed of a central design within a circle. The remainder of the chart is

divided into fourths drawn diagonally across the pillow design and marked by dark blue lines; each of these fourths is a repeat of the same design.

Canvas Size: 19″ × 19″ piece of #13 white canvas

Finished Size: 15″ × 15″ if worked on #13 canvas

Chart Thread Count: 201 wide × 201 high

Color Code (Paterna):

⊠ dark blue (334)
⊞ medium blue (385)
⊘ gold (445)
⊙ dark red (240)
☐ dark red (240) in background areas
■ light red (852)
⊡ medium green (553)
☐ cream (040) in backgrounds and small blocks

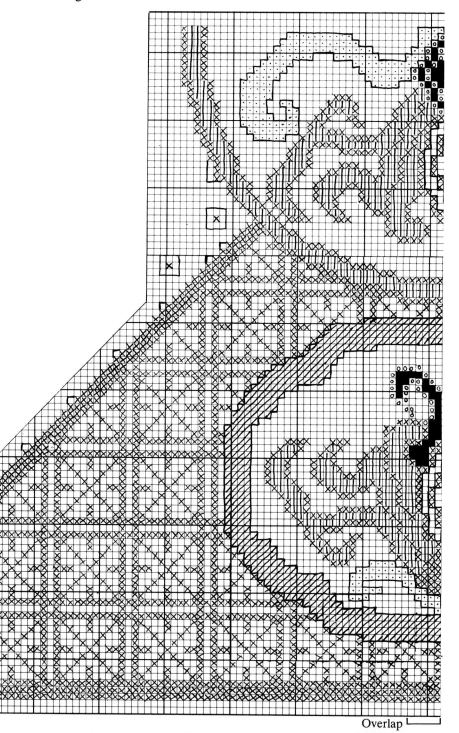

Overlap ⌐

Stitches: continental and basketweave

Instructions:

Find the center of your canvas as described on page 15.

Beginning with the center of the design, mark your canvas as explained on page 15. You are given one-half of the center circle but only one-fourth of the outer design area. When you turn the chart to mark the center section, match but do not repeat the center lines of the design. When you have marked the first section of the outer area of the chart, turn the chart 90 degrees and match the design elements marked on the right side of the design area. Continue marking by sections.

Mark the top of the canvas so you remember to work the basketweave without turning the canvas, thus insuring that all stitches slant from lower left to upper right.

Work the designs as shown on the chart in continental and basketweave (2-ply yarn), using continental for outlines and single rows of stitches and basketweave for larger areas. Try not to pull the continental too tightly along the many single rows of stitches, so the finished piece of needlepoint will not be difficult to block.

Work each of the small blocks by surrounding a stitch of dark blue with stitches of cream.

Fill in the background surrounding the blocked areas with dark red; fill in all other with cream. Refer to the photograph on page 29 as a guide to color placement in the background areas.

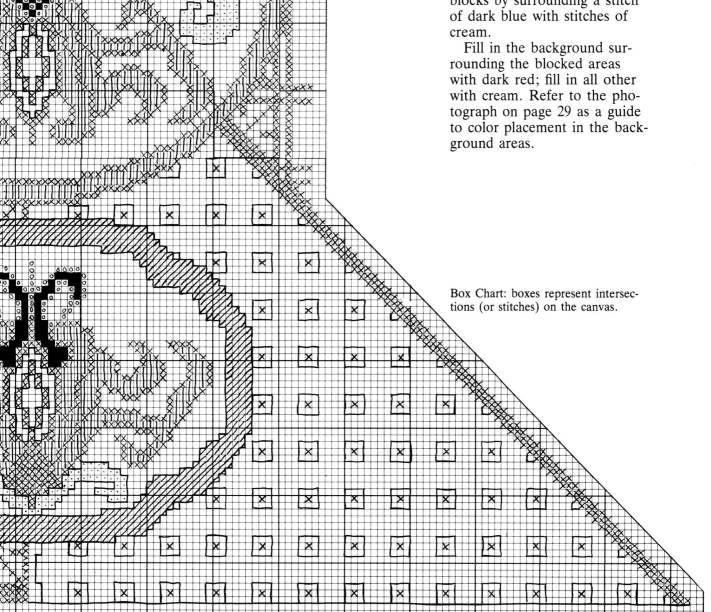

↓ Center

← Center
Do not repeat center line.

Box Chart: boxes represent intersections (or stitches) on the canvas.

└─┘ Overlap

ORIENTAL FLOWER

The pattern of this design blends happily with Imari, but the colors also make this a companion for several of the other designs in *Classics for Needlepoint.* Enjoy one design by itself, or line a sofa with pillows in a combination of the patterns with their related colors and motifs.

Canvas Size: 17″ × 15½″ piece of #13 white canvas

Finished Size: 13″ × 11½″ if worked on #13 canvas

Chart Thread Count: 175 wide × 151 high

Color Code (Paterna):
☒ dark blue (334)
■ medium blue (385)
◉ gold (445)
◩ medium green (553)
◮ medium red (850)
⊡ dark red (810)
☐ cream (040) used in background and rows of straight gobelin

Stitches: continental, basketweave, and straight gobelin with mitered corners

Instructions:

To begin marking the canvas, come in 2″ from the right and 2″ from the bottom of the canvas. This is the point for the lower right corner of the design. Allow for the placement of two rows of straight gobelin (each row over 4 threads) on both the right side and the bottom of the canvas. Mark the charted design as explained on page 15. Continue marking the repeated squares until you have marked 13 squares wide and 11 squares high.

Mark the top of the canvas so you remember to work basketweave without turning the canvas, thus insuring that all stitches slant from lower left to upper right.

Work the design in continental and basketweave (2-ply yarn), using continental for outlines and single rows of stitches and basketweave for larger areas. When you are working, remember that pulling too tightly along the many lines of continental will make the finished piece of needlepoint difficult to block.

Fill in the background areas (all the areas not marked on the chart) with cream.

The two rows of straight gobelin (over 4 threads of canvas each) on the outside of the design are optional. If you wish to use it, it should be worked last (3-ply yarn) because straight gobelin becomes fuzzy when it is handled too much. Miter the corners of the frame of straight gobelin.

Box Chart: boxes represent intersections (or stitches) on the canvas.

Continue squares for desired size.

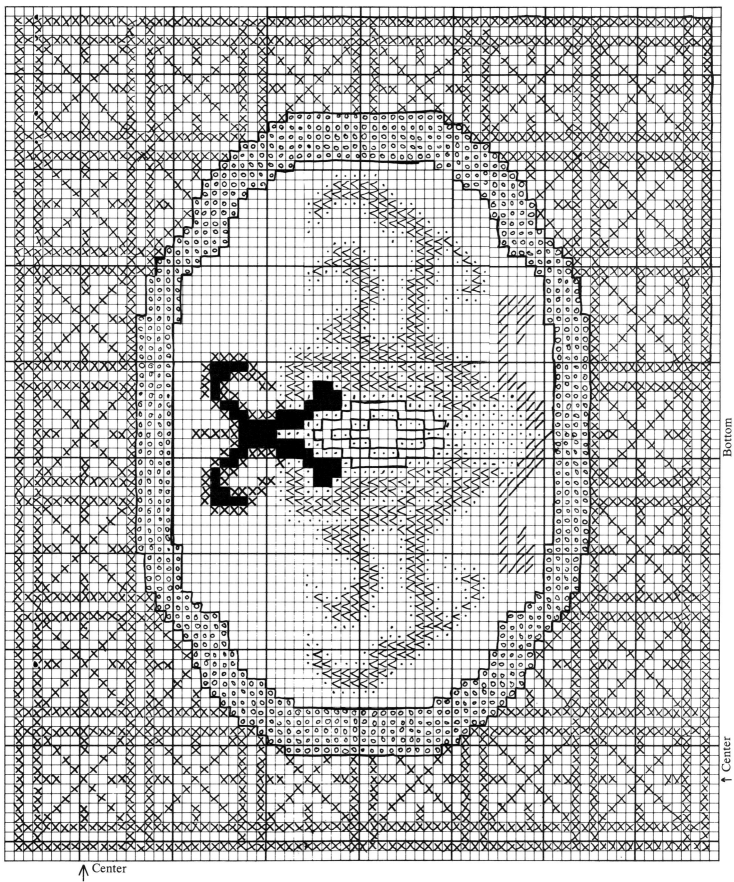

Bottom

↑ Center

↑ Center

PATTERNED IRIS

This design is less complex than it may seem at first glance. It is the background in different colors that changes the appearance of the repeated patterns. To simplify the design, not all the color areas are shown on the chart. See the instructions below for additional color placement.

Canvas Size: 18″ × 19″ piece of #13 white canvas

Finished Size: 14″ × 15″ if worked on #13 canvas

Chart Thread Count: 183 wide × 195 high

Color Code (Paterna):
- ◻ dark green (505)
- ⊙ medium green (555)
- ◭ light green (570)
- ▪ dark coral (215)
- ⊠ medium coral (273)
- ◻ medium coral (273) in lower background area
- ◻ light coral (R78) inside flower petals and in upper background area
- ◻ cream (040) in center background area

Stitches: continental and basketweave

Instructions:

Come in two inches from the bottom and left of your canvas, and mark the canvas according to the instructions on page 15.

Mark the top of your canvas so you remember to work basketweave without turning the canvas, thus insuring that all stitches slant from lower left to upper right.

Work all the marked areas (2-ply yarn throughout), using continental for outlines and single rows of stitches and basketweave for larger areas.

Work the unmarked areas inside the flower petals in light coral.

Work the unmarked background area in three different colors, referring to the color code and the photograph on page 5.

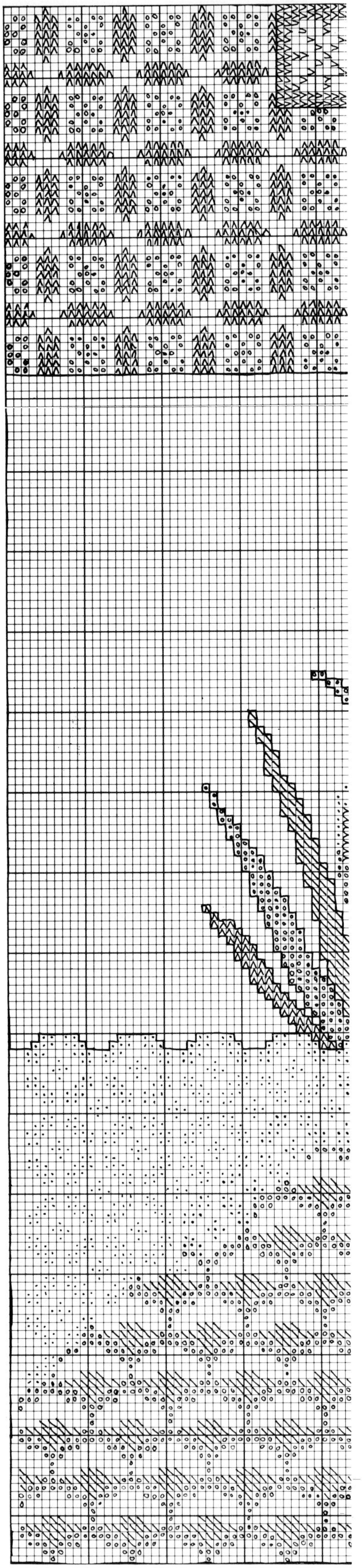

Box Chart: boxes represent intersections (or stitches) on the canvas.

Not all color areas are indicated; see accompanying instructions.

Center

Center

IRIS COMPANION

This design uses the corals and creams in Patterned Iris in a small floral motif surrounded by wide patterned borders. To simplify the chart, not all the color areas are shown on the chart. See the instructions below for additional color placement.

Canvas Size: 22″ × 17″ piece of #13 white canvas

Finished Size: 18″ × 13″ if worked on #13 canvas

Chart Thread Count: 234 wide × 171 high

Color Code (Paterna):
- ☒ medium green (510)
- ☐ medium green (510) in rows of straight gobelin
- ■ dark coral (215)
- ⊙ medium coral (273)
- ☐ medium coral (273) in inner border and in rows of straight gobelin
- ☐ light coral (R78) to fill in flower design
- ☐ cream (040) background

Stitches: continental, basketweave, straight gobelin with mitered corners, and back stitch (optional)

Instructions:

Find the center of your canvas as described on page 15.

Beginning with the center of the design, mark your canvas as explained on page 15. Be sure to leave the exact number of threads designated for the straight gobelin: 4 threads for each row. In marking the latticed inner border, notice that there is a double center on the long side. This makes an irregular pattern in the center.

Mark the top of the canvas so you remember to work basketweave without turning the canvas, thus insuring that all stitches slant from lower left to upper right. Work all areas except those marked for straight gobelin in continental and basketweave (2-ply yarn). Use continental for outlines and single rows of stitches and basketweave for larger areas.

Not all areas are marked for color. The flower motif in the center should be filled in with light coral. The background of the center motif is cream. After working the medium green of the latticed inner border, fill in the remaining area with medium coral. The background of the outer border is cream.

Work two rows of straight gobelin (each row over 4 threads) beyond the charted area. The inside row is medium coral and the outside row is medium green. Refer to the photograph on page 6.

Work the rows of straight gobelin (3-ply yarn) last since they tend to become fuzzy when they are handled too much; miter the corners.

To make a neater finish, you may use a back stitch (1-ply yarn) between the rows of straight gobelin.

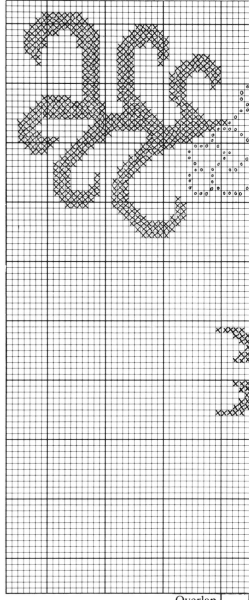

Overlap

Straight gobelin with mitered corners ⌐ Medium coral
⌐ Medium green
⌐ Medium coral

Straight gobelin with mitered corners — Medium coral

Center ←

⌐▭⌐ Overlap ↑ Center

Box Chart: boxes represent intersections (or stitches) on the canvas.

Not all color areas are indicated; see accompanying instructions.

LATTICE & FLOWERS

This companion to two other latticed designs has an interesting scalloped shape. Work the design as it is shown, or vary the pattern by working only the central area and filling in the border area with a solid color.

To simplify the chart, not all color areas are marked. See the instructions below for additional color placement.

Canvas Size: 20″ × 18″ piece of #13 white canvas

Finished Size: 16″ × 14″ if worked on #13 canvas

Chart Thread Count: 209 wide × 183 high

Color Code (Paterna):
- ◻ dark coral (242)
- ⊠ medium coral (852)
- ☐ medium coral (852) in four-way bargello flowers
- ⊡ light coral (853)
- ⊘ dark green (540)
- ☐ medium green (553) in boxed area and inside leaves
- ☐ cream (040) in background

Stitches: continental, basketweave, and four-way bargello

Instructions:
Find the center of your canvas as described on page 15.

Beginning with the center of the design, mark the canvas as explained on page 15. You are given one-half of the pattern. Rotate your canvas and con-tinue marking to complete the design. Do not repeat the center line.

Work the four-way bargello flowers (3-ply yarn) as indicated by the chart; notice that the chart gives a line, or stitch, pattern for the flower.

Work the bargello flowers shown in the line chart around the flower centers marked on the main chart. Along the edges of the design, only a portion of the flower is used.

Mark the top of the canvas so you remember to work basketweave without turning the canvas, thus insuring that all stitches slant from lower left to upper right. Use continental and basketweave stitches (2-ply yarn) in the remainder of the design. Use continental for outlines and single rows of stitches and basketweave for larger areas.

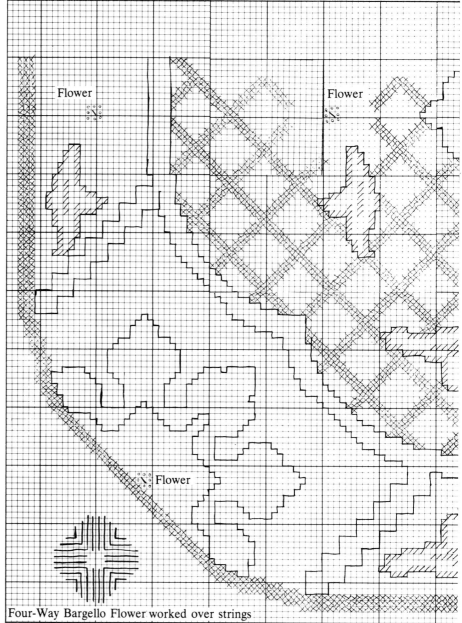

Four-Way Bargello Flower worked over strings

Overlap ⌐

Work the marked areas of your canvas.

Fill in the leaves and boxed areas with medium green; refer to the photograph on page 17 if you are not sure of placement.

Work the background in cream. Work 6 rows beyond the coral border so the coral border is not lost in finishing. These extra rows are included in the chart thread count.

Box Chart: boxes represent intersections (or stitches) on the canvas.

Not all color areas are indicated; see accompanying instructions.

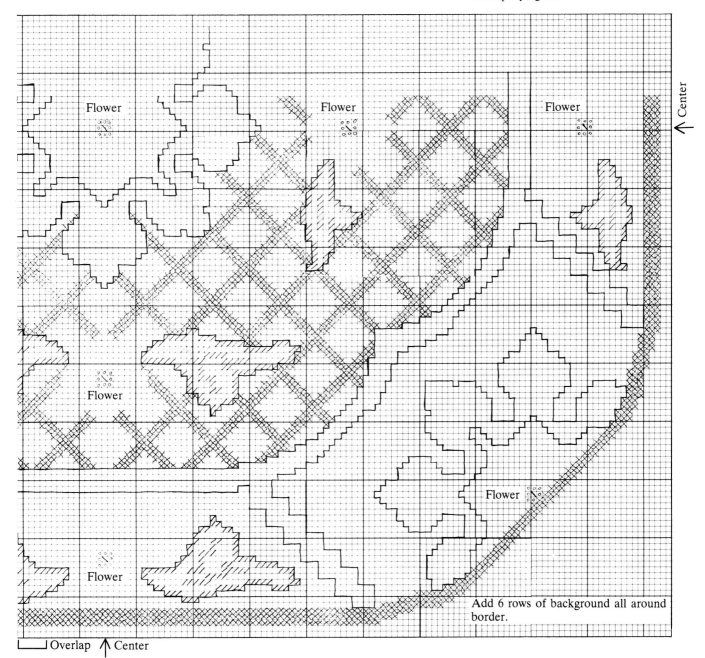

Flower

Flower

Flower

Flower

Flower

Flower

Center

Add 6 rows of background all around border.

Overlap   Center

LATTICE & TULIPS

Stylized tulips and lattice are surrounded by rows of straight gobelin in a particularly orderly design. The chart provides the main lines of the designs, but follow the instructions below to fill in some of the areas not shown on the chart.

Canvas Size: 19½″ × 19½″ piece of #13 white canvas

Finished Size: 15½″ × 15½″ if worked on #13 canvas

Chart Thread Count: 203 wide × 203 high

Color Code (Paterna):
◧ dark coral (242)
☐ dark coral (242) in rows of straight gobelin
⊠ medium coral (852)
☐ medium coral (852) in rows of straight gobelin
⊡ light coral (853)
☐ light coral (853) in rows of straight gobelin
⊡ dark green (540)
■ medium green (553)
☐ medium green (553) inside leaves
☐ cream (040) in background

Stitches: continental, basketweave, straight gobelin with mitered corners, and back stitch (optional)

Instructions:
Find the center of your canvas as described on page 15.

You have been given one-fourth of the pattern. Beginning with the center of the design, mark this section as explained on page 15. Then rotate your canvas and continue marking to complete the full design. Do not repeat the center lines. Be sure to leave the exact number of threads of canvas designated for the straight gobelin: 4 threads for each row for a total of 12 between design areas and another 12 at the outside edges.

Except for the area marked for straight gobelin, the design is worked in continental and basketweave (2-ply yarn). Use continental for outlines and single rows of stitches and basketweave for larger areas. Mark the top of the canvas so you remember to work basketweave without turning the canvas, thus insuring that all stitches slant from lower left to upper right.

Work the marked areas.

Fill in the leaves with medium green.

Fill in the background with cream.

Work the rows of straight gobelin (3-ply yarn); miter the corners. Back stitch (1-ply yarn) between the rows of straight gobelin if you wish; this is not necessary, but it makes a neater finish.

Work three rows of straight gobelin (each row over 4 threads) beyond the charted area. The inside row is dark coral, the middle row is medium coral, and the outside row is light coral. Refer to the photograph on page 19.

Box Chart: boxes represent intersections (or stitches) on the canvas.

Not all color areas are indicated; see accompanying instructions.

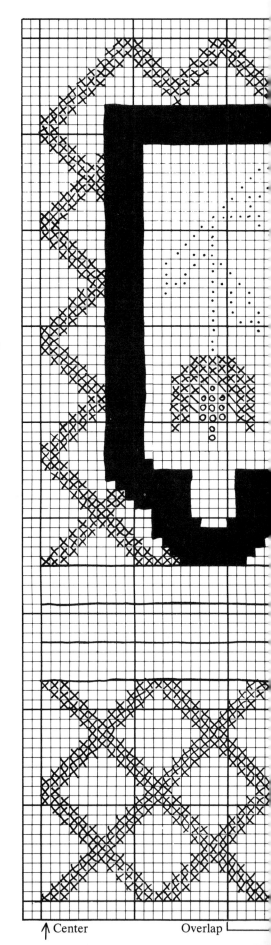

↑ Center   Overlap ⌐

Center
Do not repeat center line.

Light coral

Medium coral

Straight gobelin with mitered corners

Dark coral

Overlap

LATTICE & LACE

One of three striking companion designs, this can be enjoyed separately or in a combination of colors and patterns. This chart was made for easy marking and counting; the sections of the design that are worked in green have been outlined rather than completely marked.

Canvas Size: 18″ × 18″ piece of #13 white canvas

Finished Size: 14″ × 14″ if worked on #13 canvas

Chart Thread Count: 187 wide × 187 high

Color Code (Paterna):
- ◿ light coral (853)
- ☐ light coral (853) in rows of straight gobelin
- ☒ medium coral (852)
- ☐ medium coral (852) in four-way flower and rows of straight gobelin
- ⊡ medium green (553)
- ☐ medium green (553) in unmarked areas of design
- ☐ dark coral (242) in rows of straight gobelin
- ☐ cream (040) in background

Stitches: four-way bargello, continental, basketweave, straight gobelin with mitered corners, and back stitch (optional)

Instructions:

Find the center of your canvas as described on page 15.

Beginning with the center of the design, mark your canvas as explained on page 15. The chart gives one-fourth of the design. Rotate your canvas and continue marking to complete the design. Do not repeat the center line. When marking, be sure to leave the exact number of rows required for the straight gobelin stitch: 4 threads for each row for a total of 12 between design areas and another 12 at the outside edges.

Work the bargello flowers shown in the line chart around the flower centers marked on the main chart. Along the edges of the design, only a portion of the flower is used.

Mark the top of the canvas so you remember to work basketweave without turning the canvas, thus insuring that all stitches slant from lower left to upper right. Work the latticed areas with continental and basketweave (2-ply yarn), using continental for outlines and single rows of stitches and basketweave for larger areas. Fill in the areas outlined with green with more yarn in the same shade of green. Fill in the cream background.

Work three rows of straight gobelin (each row over 4 threads) beyond the charted area. The inside row is dark coral, the middle row is medium coral, and the outside row is light coral. Refer to the photograph on page 20.

Work the rows of straight gobelin (3-ply) last since they tend to become fuzzy when handled too much; miter the corners. You may wish to work rows of back stitch (1-ply yarn) for a neat finish between the rows of straight gobelin.

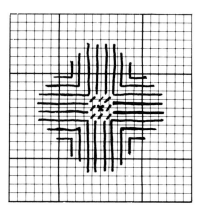

Four-Way Bargello Flower Pattern: worked over strings, not intersections.

Box Chart: boxes represent intersections (or stitches) on the canvas.

Not all color areas are indicated; see accompanying instructions.

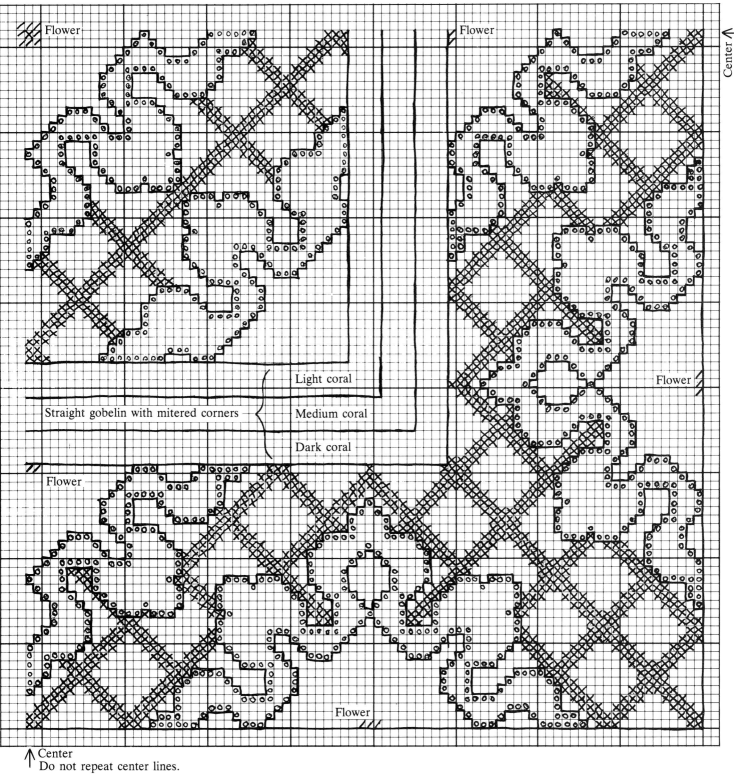

Flower

Flower

Light coral

Straight gobelin with mitered corners { Medium coral

Dark coral

Flower

Flower

Flower

Center
Do not repeat center lines.

MUSEUM

This bold motif is a part of a larger design created especially for a rug made for the Columbus, Georgia, Museum of Art. This is one of the easier charts to begin marking because it is done on #10 canvas and because the design itself is fairly simple.

Canvas Size: 19½″ × 19½″ piece of #10 white canvas

Finished Size (including border): 15½″ × 15½″ if worked on #10 canvas

Chart Thread Count: 157 wide × 157 high

Color Code (Paterna):
- ▨ rust (215)
- ⊡ green (559)
- ◩ gold (445)
- ◪ light blue (395)
- ⊠ dark blue (334)
- ☐ dark blue (334) in background
- ☐ cream (040) in background

Stitches: continental and basketweave

Instructions:

Find the center of your canvas as described on page 15.

Beginning in the center of the design, mark your canvas as explained on page 15. The chart shows one-half of the center pattern and one-fourth of the border. Rotate your canvas and continue marking to complete the design. Do not repeat the center line.

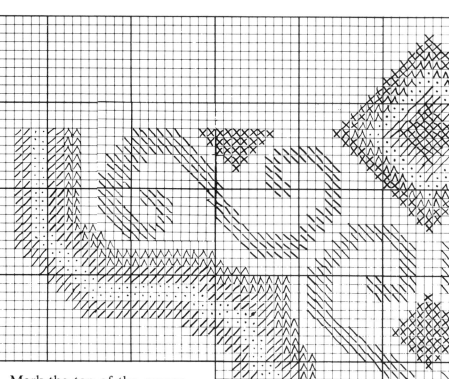

Mark the top of the canvas so you remember to work basketweave without turning the canvas, thus insuring that all stitches slant from lower left to upper right.

Work the entire design in continental and basketweave (2-ply yarn). Use continental for outlines and single rows of stitches and basketweave for larger areas. Fill in the background within the central motif in cream. Fill in the background between the central motif and border in dark blue; then fill in the background of the border in cream.

Box Chart: boxes represent intersections (or stitches) on the canvas.

Not all color areas are indicated; see accompanying instructions.

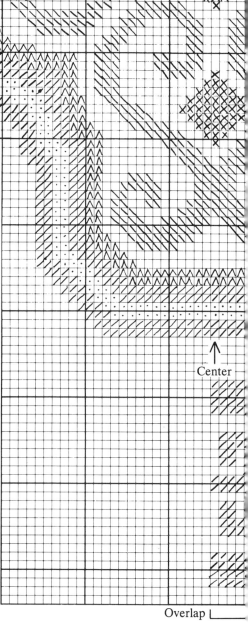

Center

Overlap

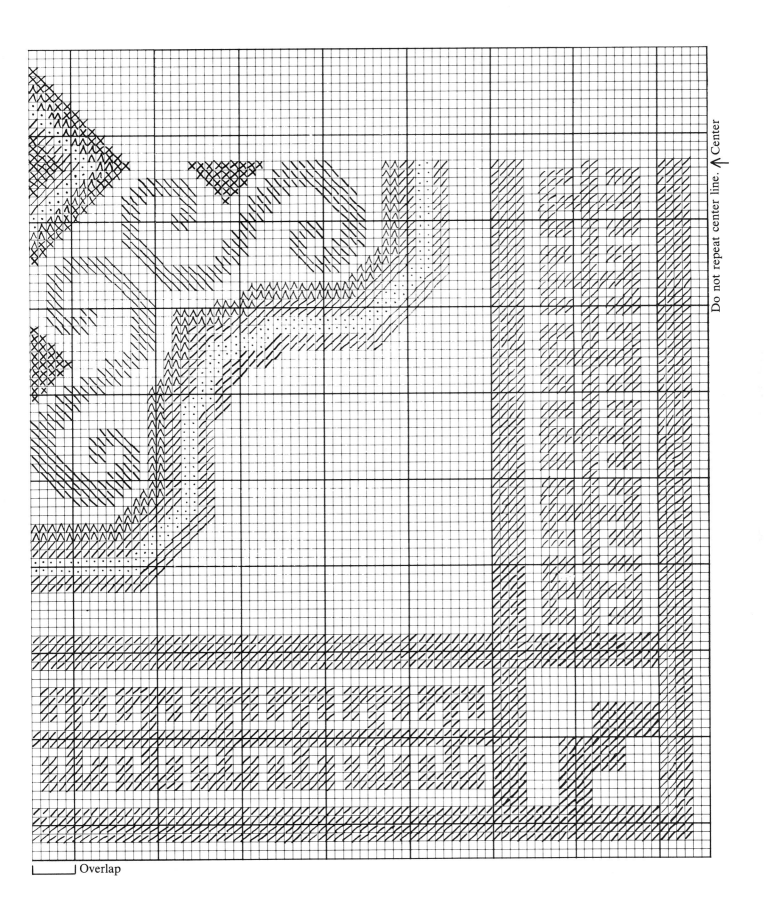

Overlap

BACKGAMMON

My backgammon board is designed for actual play. You may want to have it blocked and backed with felt by a professional. It is rolled for easy storage; folding would break the threads.

Canvas Size: 27″ × 18″ piece of #13 white canvas

Finished Size: 23″ × 14″ if worked on #13 canvas

Chart Thread Count: 303 wide × 183 high

Color Code (Paterna):
- ◻ dark rust (215)
- ☐ medium rust (273) in points on board and inside flowers of border motif
- ⊠ black (050)
- ⊡ dark gold (433)
- ☐ light gold (453) in points on board
- ☐ cream (040) in background area marked off with black squares and around playing area
- ☐ black (050) in background areas that frame the playing area

Stitches: continental and basketweave

Instructions:

Find the center of your canvas as described on page 15.

Beginning in the center of the design, mark your canvas as explained on page 15. Mark the lower right section just as it is shown on the chart. This will be one-fourth of the total design. Repeat the design. Refer to the photograph on page 72 to check color placement. For the opposite side of the board, turn the chart upside down and draw so the points opposite each other on the board are different colors.

Mark the top of the canvas so you remember to work basketweave without turning the canvas, thus insuring that all stitches slant from lower left to upper right.

Work the marked areas in continental and basketweave (2-ply yarn), using continental for outlines and single rows of stitches and basketweave for larger areas. Be sure not to pull the continental too tightly along the black lines in the

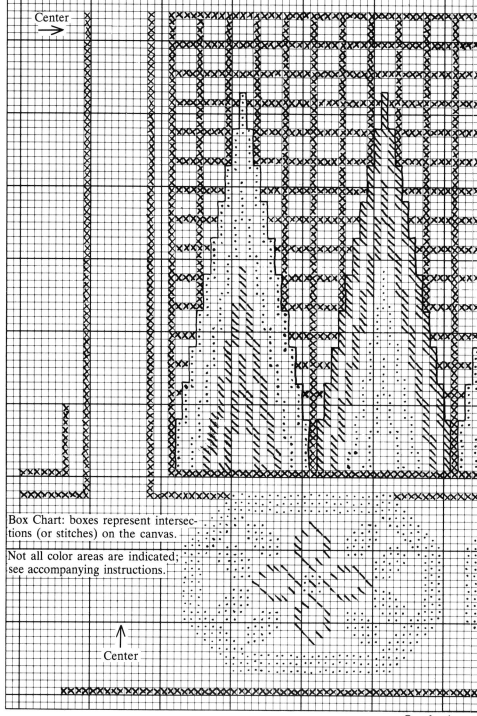

Center →

Box Chart: boxes represent intersections (or stitches) on the canvas.

Not all color areas are indicated; see accompanying instructions.

↑ Center

Overlap ⌐

center section, or the finished piece will be difficult to block.

Fill in between the two rows of dark rust in the first point on the lower right with medium rust. Add one row of medium rust between the inside row of dark rust and the row of dark gold. Fill in the remaining open area of the point with light gold.

Reverse the patterns of rust and gold for the next point. Continue to alternate the patterns across the board.

Fill in the background within the black squares with cream.

Fill in flowers in the border motifs with medium rust.

Fill in the backgrounds within the border motifs with cream.

Work two rows of cream to surround the halves of playing surface.

Work the remaining border area in black.

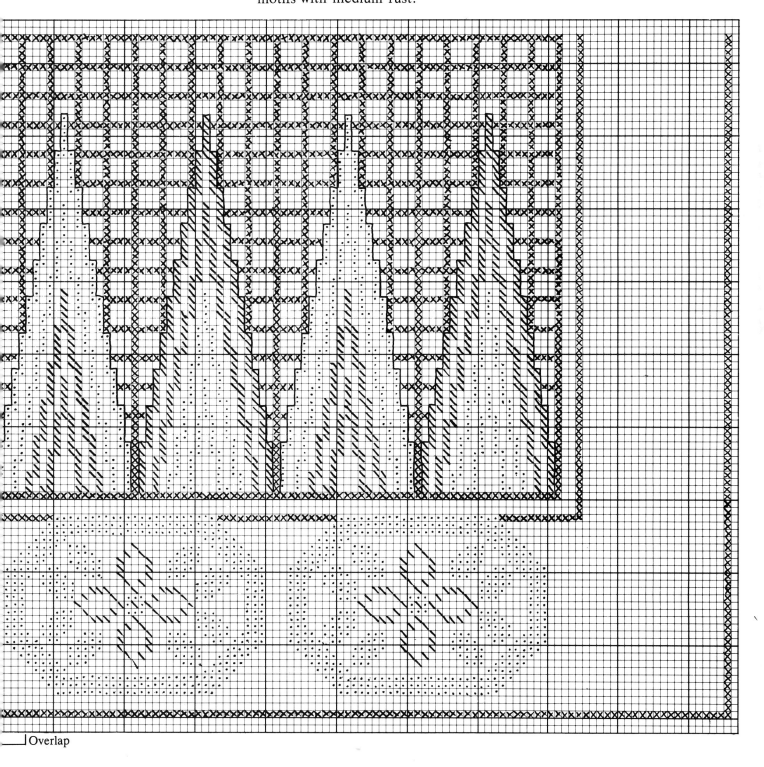

Overlap

SUMMER LOTUS

These chair seats are among the simplest designs to mark onto canvas because the design areas are all outlined in medium gold and filled in with various colors. The two related patterns allow you to co-ordinate side chairs and arm chairs.

It is necessary to measure carefully for chair seats. For slip seats, it is usually adequate to draw a pattern the size of the seat, add 1″ of worked area to fold under the seat, and allow 2″ of canvas beyond this for attaching to the underside of the seat. For any chair seat more complicated than the slip seat, it is a good idea to take the chair to an upholsterer who can draw a pattern for the needlepoint. Arm chairs, particularly, can be a problem because the arms may be attached to the seat in any number of ways.

Buy all the yarn you will need at one time so you do not have problems with matching dye lots.

When the chair seat is finished, instruct the upholsterer not to cut into the needlepoint.

Greens and corals are used in the chair seats shown in the photographs on page 75, but these colors can be changed to fit the color scheme of your dining room.

Arm Chairs

Canvas and Finished Size: Determined by the size of your chair. Use #13 white canvas.

Color Code (Paterna):
- ▨ medium gold (445)
- ⊡ dark coral (952)
- ⊞ medium coral (972)
- ☐ dark green (510) in geometric design
- ☐ medium green (555) in leaves and stems
- ☐ cream (040) in background

Stitches: continental and basketweave.

Instructions:

Find the center of your canvas as explained on page 15.

Beginning with the center of the design, mark your canvas as explained on page 15. The chart for the arm chairs gives half of the center section and a fourth of the outer section. When you turn your canvas to mark the center section, match but do not repeat the center lines of the design.

Mark the top of your canvas so you remember to work basketweave without turning the canvas, thus insuring that all stitches slant from lower left to upper right. Work all of the design in continental and basketweave (2-ply yarn), using continental for outlines and single rows of stitches and basketweave for larger areas.

Work all the gold outlines shown on the chart.

Fill in the other marked areas on the chart.

Fill in the remaining area of the geometric pattern with dark green.

Fill in leaves and stems with medium green.

Work the background in cream.

Box Chart: boxes represent intersections (or stitches) on the canvas.

Not all color areas are indicated; see accompanying instructions.

← Center
Do not repeat center line.

↑ Center

Side Chairs

Canvas and Finished Size: Determined by the size of your chair. Use #13 white canvas.

Color Code (Paterna):

- ☑ medium gold (445)
- ☐ dark green (510) in base of flower and attached scroll design
- ☐ medium green (555) in leaves and stems
- ⊡ dark coral (952)
- ☐ medium coral (972) in petals of flower and part of geometric design
- ☐ cream (040) in background

Stitches: continental and basketweave

Instructions:

Find the center of your canvas as explained on page 15.

Beginning with the center of the design, mark your canvas as explained on page 15. You are given all of the design for the side chairs.

Mark the top of your canvas so you remember to work basketweave without turning the canvas, thus insuring that all stitches slant from lower left to upper right. Work all of the design in continental and basketweave (2-ply yarn), using continental for outlines and single rows of stitches and basketweave for larger areas.

Work all the gold outlines shown on the chart.

Fill in the areas marked for dark coral.

Fill in the remainder of the geometric pattern with medium coral.

Fill in the base of the flower and attached scroll pattern with dark green.

Fill in the remaining flower petals with medium coral.

Fill in the stems and leaves with medium green.

Work the background in cream.

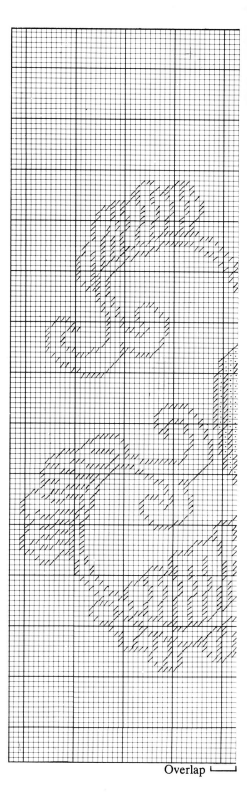

Box Chart: boxes represent intersections (or stitches) on the canvas.

Not all color areas are indicated; see accompanying instructions.

Overlap ⌐

COUNTRY GARDEN

Reminiscent of the grace of a country garden, this pattern is one of the simpler ones to count and mark. The size of the canvas will be determined by the size of your chair. For a simple slip seat, it is usually adequate to measure the size of the seat, allow 1″ of needlepoint to fold under the seat, and add 2″ of empty canvas on each side. For a seat more complicated than the slip seat, it is a good idea to have an upholsterer cut a pattern for the needlepoint. Arms of chairs, particularly, may be difficult to plan for. Buy all the yarn you will need at one time so you do not have problems with matching dye lots. When the chair seat is finished, instruct the upholsterer not to cut into the needlepoint. To simplify the chart, not all color areas are indicated; read the instructions below for additional color placement.

If you do not need chair seats, you may enjoy a pillow with this pattern. A pillow 15″ square will include the pattern and 1″ of background beyond if you use #13 canvas.

Canvas and Finished Size for Chair Seats: Determined by size of chair. Use #13 white canvas.

Canvas Size for Pillow: 19″ × 19″ piece of #13 white canvas

Finished Size of Pillow: 15″ × 15″ if worked on #13 canvas

Chart Thread Count for Pillow: 180 wide × 180 high

Color Code (Paterna):
◩ aqua (793)
☐ aqua (793) in background
⊡ dark coral (852)
☐ light coral (853) in flowers
☒ medium green (553)
☐ light green (593) in leaves
☐ cream (040) in background

Stitches: continental and basketweave

Instructions:
Find the center of your canvas as described on page 15.

Beginning with the center of the design, mark your canvas as explained on page 15. You are given the full center section of the chart and one-fourth of the outside sections. Rotate your canvas to complete the pattern.

Mark the top of your canvas so you remember to work basketweave without turning the canvas, thus insuring that all stitches slant from lower left to upper right. Work all areas in continental and basketweave (2-ply yarn), using continental for outlines and single rows of stitches and basketweave for larger areas.

Work the marked areas.

Fill in the flowers with light coral.

Fill in the leaves with light green.

Refer to the photographs on page 76 for placement of cream and aqua in the background; the appearance changes drastically with the use of a different color in the background.

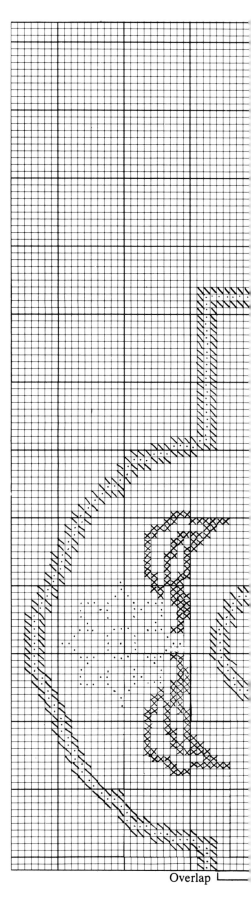

Overlap

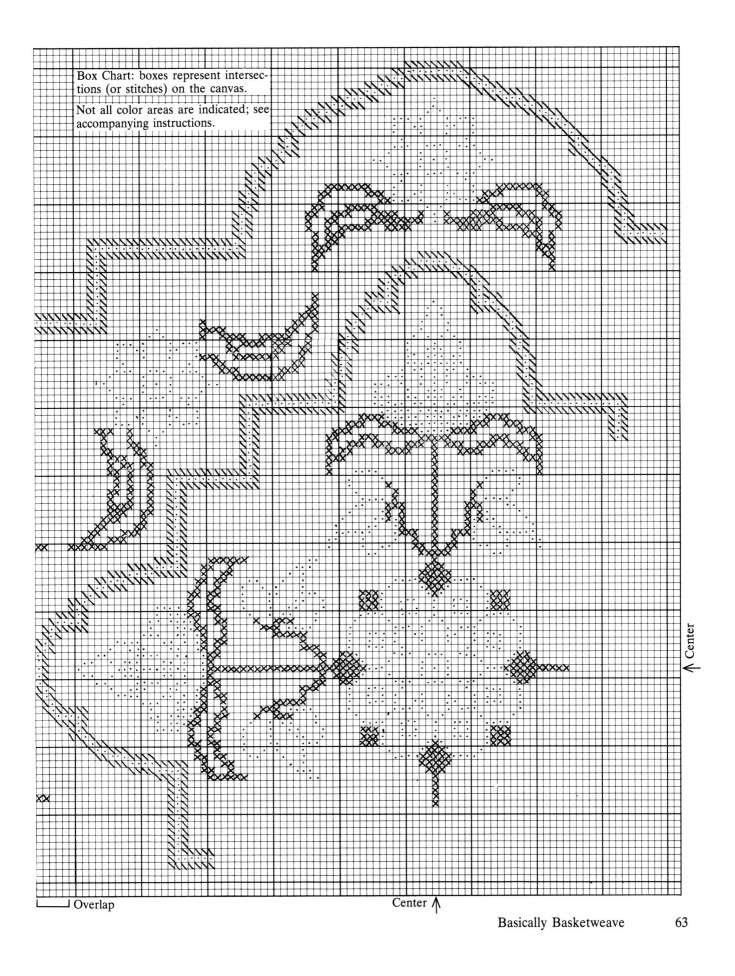

Box Chart: boxes represent intersections (or stitches) on the canvas.

Not all color areas are indicated; see accompanying instructions.

Overlap

Center

Center

BAMBOO

Bamboo, the Chinese symbol for longevity, is set against a background of geometric design. This pattern would be lovely in a combination of shades of any single color.

Canvas Size: 15″ × 17″ piece of #13 white canvas

Finished Size: 11″ × 13″ if worked on #13 canvas

Chart Thread Count: 149 wide × 170 high

Color Code (Paterna):
- ■ dark green (505)
- ◪ medium green (510)
- ◎ light green (570)
- ☐ cream (040) in background

Stitches: continental and basketweave

Instructions:

To begin marking your canvas as explained on page 15, come in 2″ from the bottom edge and 2″ from the left edge of the canvas. Begin here to mark the background pattern, working from bottom left diagonally across the canvas.

After the pattern is marked onto your canvas, mark the top of the canvas so you remember to work basketweave without turning the canvas, thus insuring that all stitches slant from lower left to upper right. All the design is worked in a combination of continental and basketweave stitches (2-ply yarn), using continental for outlines and single rows of stitches and basketweave for larger areas.

Box Chart: boxes represent intersections (or stitches) on the canvas.

Bottom

CHINESE SYMBOL FOR SUCCESS

A brush, ink cake, and scepter are combined into a rebus meaning "May your wishes be fulfilled." The complete design is composed of a charted area worked in continental and basketweave and surrounded by a row of straight gobelin and a bargello border.

Canvas Size: 17″ × 15½″ piece of #13 white canvas

Finished Size (including bargello border): 13″ × 11½″ if worked on #13 canvas

Chart Thread Count: 168 wide × 152 high

Color Code (Paterna):
⊠ dark blue (334)
☐ dark blue (334) in row of straight gobelin
⊡ medium blue (385)
■ light blue (395)
⊙ dark red (810)
☐ light red (850) inside dark red outlines
⊘ dark gold (433)
☐ light gold (453) inside dark gold outlines
☐ cream (040) in background

Stitches: continental, basketweave, straight gobelin with mitered corners, and bargello

Instructions:
Find the center of your canvas as described on page 15.

Beginning with the center of the design, mark your canvas as explained on page 15.

Mark the top of the canvas so you remember to work basketweave without turning the canvas, thus insuring that all stitches slant from lower left to upper right. The rows of straight gobelin and the bargello border will be worked in four directions.

Use continental and basketweave (2-ply yarn) in all the area of the central design. Use continental for outlines and single rows of stitches and basketweave for larger areas.

Work the marked areas of the design.

Fill in the areas outlined by dark red with light red.

Fill in the areas outlined by dark gold with light gold.

Work the background in cream.

Allow 4 threads of canvas for working the row of straight gobelin between the design area and border.

Before working the straight gobelin, work the bargello border that is shown on page 118.

Work the row of straight gobelin (3-ply yarn) over 4 threads in dark blue; miter the corners. This is worked last because it may become fuzzy if handled too much.

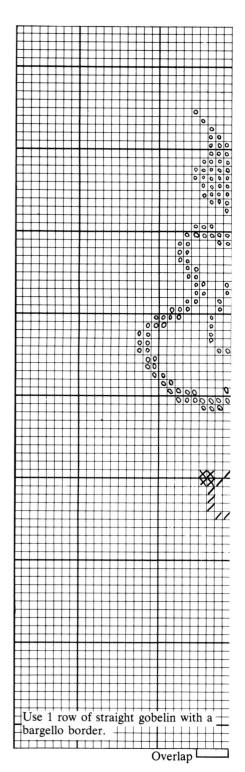

Use 1 row of straight gobelin with a bargello border.

Overlap

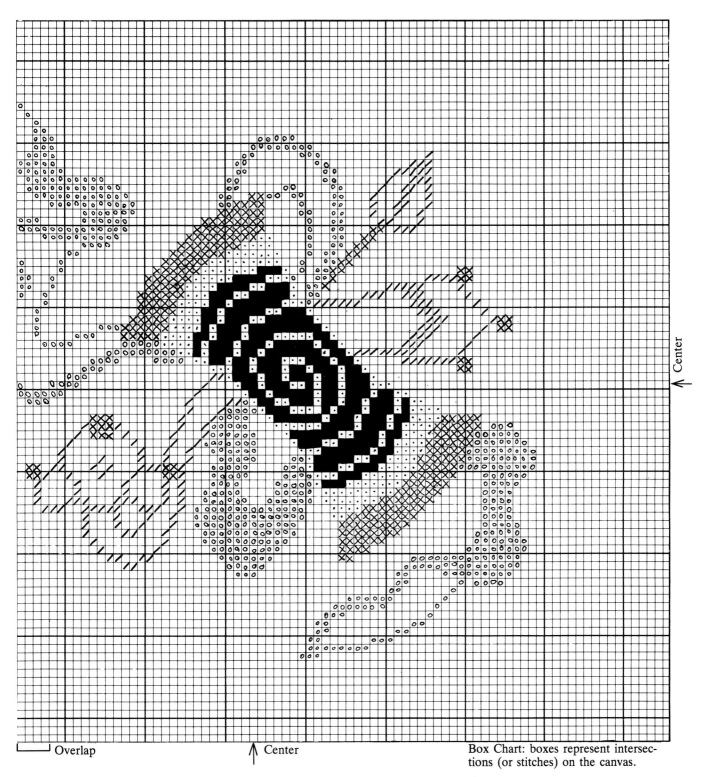

└─┘ Overlap   ↑ Center

Box Chart: boxes represent intersections (or stitches) on the canvas.

Not all color areas are indicated; see
accompanying instructions.

Basically Basketweave   67

BLUE CLOUD BAND

Clouds, denoting beneficial rain and fertility, surround a geometric motif in this simple but effective pattern.

Canvas Size: 13″ × 13″ piece of #13 white canvas

Finished Size: 9″ × 9″ if worked on #13 canvas

Chart Thread Count: 123 wide × 123 high

Color Code (Paterna):
⊠ dark blue (334)
⊙ medium blue (385)
⊘ light blue (395)
☐ cream (040) in background

Stitches: continental and basketweave

Instructions:

Find the center of your canvas as described on page 15.

You have been given one-fourth of the pattern with center marks indicated. Beginning in the center, mark your canvas as described on page 15. Turn your canvas and continue marking until the design is complete, being careful to align but not to repeat the center lines of the design.

Mark the top of the canvas so you remember to work basketweave without turning the canvas, thus insuring that all stitches slant from lower left to upper right. Work in continental and basketweave (2-ply yarn), using continental for outlines and single rows of stitches and basketweave for larger areas.

Box Chart: boxes represent intersections (or stitches) on the canvas.

Center →

Center

Blue Cloud Band, chart on page 68.

Museum, chart on page 54.

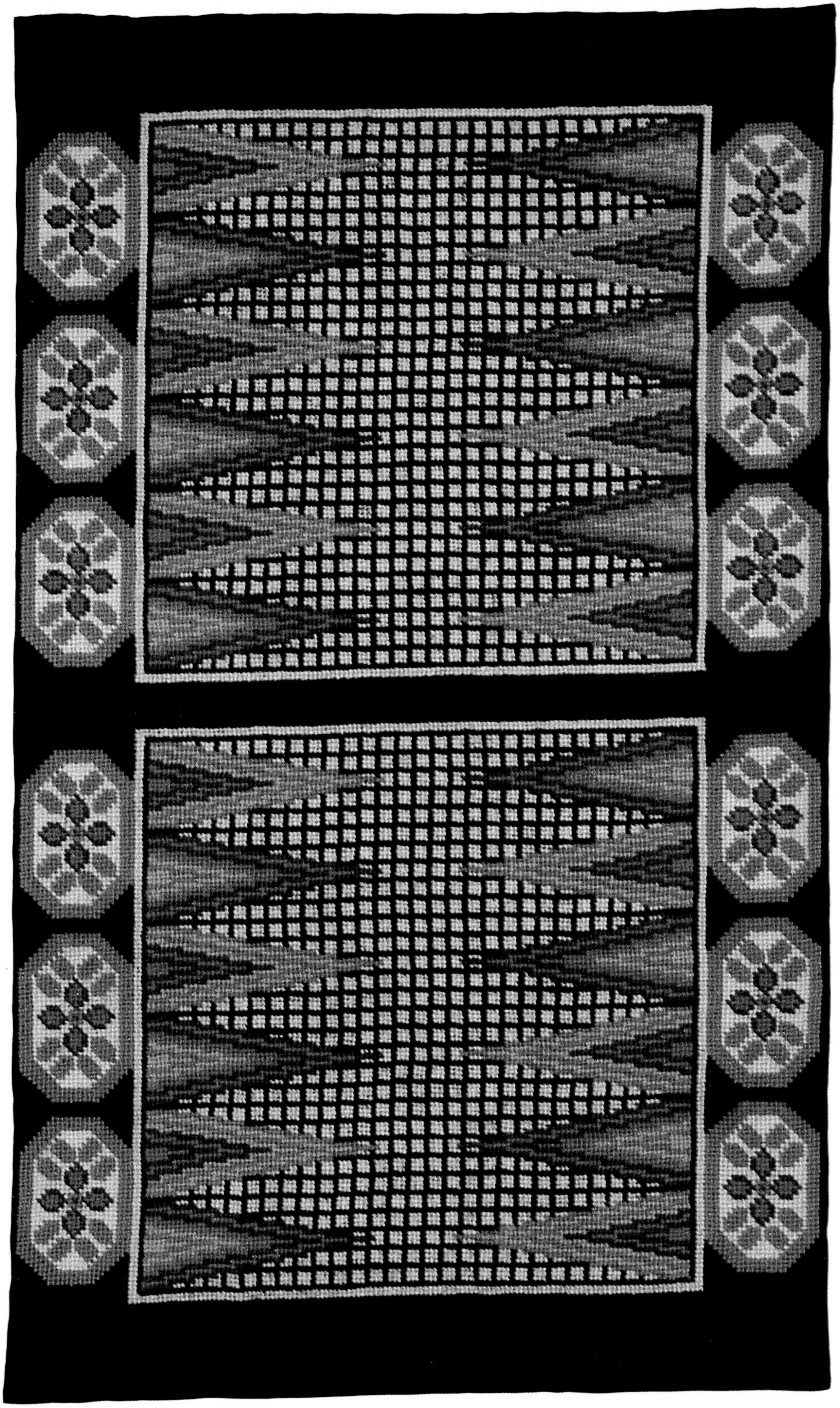

Above: Black & White Shells, chart on page 90.

Left: Backgammon, chart on page 56.

*Summer Lotus Side Chair,
chart on page 60.*

*Summer Lotus Arm Chair,
chart on page 58.*

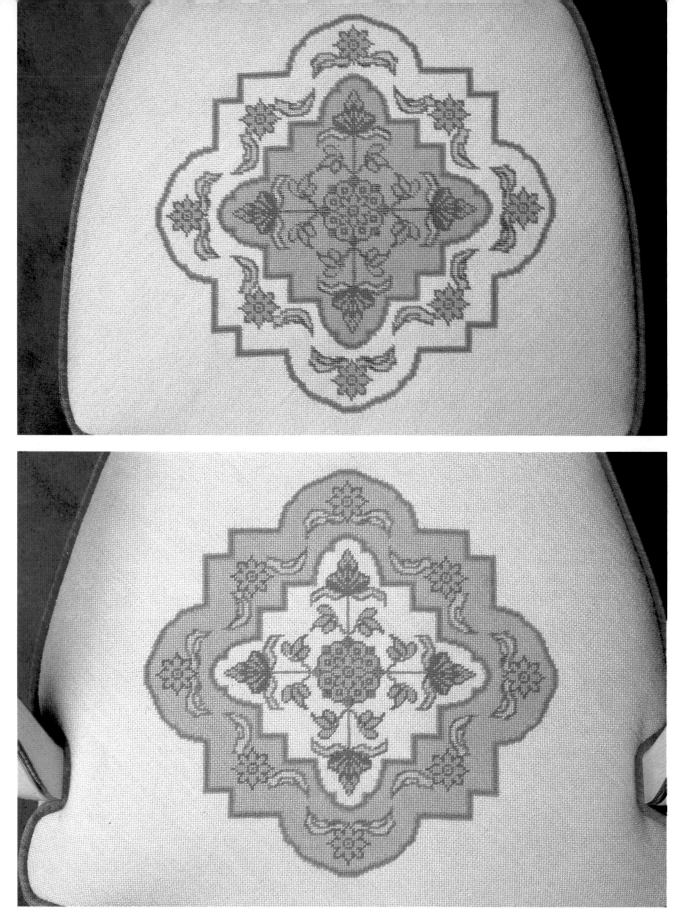

Country Garden, chart on page 62.

Basketweave
Plus

Basketweave "plus" carefully placed decorative stitches makes this group of designs particularly striking because of the unexpected textural effects: a flower in diagonal mosaic, a kaleidoscope set into a textured background, a seashell resting on textured sand, bargello borders. Any of these areas that are worked in other stitches could, of course, be worked in basketweave if you prefer, but the varying textures add interest to the work and to the finished product.

The charts show the colors of stitches but not the kinds of stitches. The directions for placement of stitches are given in the instructions that accompany each chart. All the stitches used are diagrammed and explained in the Portfolio of Stitches, page 21. Use white canvas with these designs so they can be marked by my count and mark technique explained on page 15.

LOTUS BLOSSOM

A rectangular design with its stylized and symmetrical motif blends a curlique background with a pattern of diamonds. The major design area is marked and worked in continental and basketweave from a chart that shows color area. The border area is worked from a chart of stitches in a bargello arrangement.

Canvas Size: 22″ × 18″ piece of #13 white canvas

Finished Size: 18″ × 14″ if worked on #13 canvas

Chart Thread Count: 231 wide × 184 high

Color Code (Paterna):
- ☒ dark blue (334)
- ☐ dark blue (334) in border and in rows of straight gobelin
- ◉ medium blue (385)
- ◿ medium green (553)
- ◺ dark red (810)
- ⊡ light red (850)
- ◥ dark gold (433)
- ☐ light gold (453) to fill in flower motif
- ☐ cream (040) in background of major design area
- ☐ cream (040) in border

Stitches: continental, basketweave, straight gobelin with mitered corners, and bargello

Instructions:
(Note: The chart for the central design area, which is worked *before* the border, appears on page 80.)

Find the center of your canvas as described on page 15.

Beginning in the center of the design, mark the central design area as explained on page 15. You have been given more than one-half of the main pattern. When this has been marked, rotate your canvas and mark the second half, matching but not repeating the center lines.

Mark the top of your canvas so you remember to work all basketweave without turning the canvas, thus insuring that all stitches slant from lower left to upper right. Work the central design in continental and basketweave (2-ply yarn), using continental for outlines and single rows of stitches and basketweave for larger areas.

Within the dark gold outlines, fill in with light gold. Work the background in cream.

↓ Center

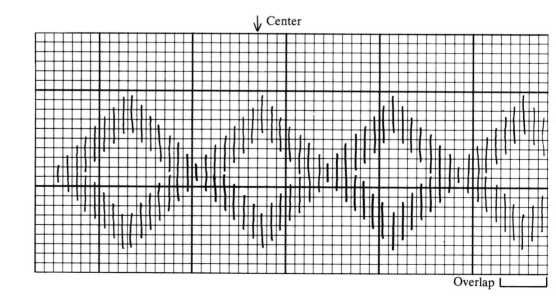

Overlap

Center →

To add the border, match the centers of the border pattern to the centers of the central design. The border pattern shows the length and pattern of the stitches and the colors (straight lines in cream, wavy lines in dark blue). You are given slightly more than one-fourth of the border. Be careful to continue the lines rather than repeating them when you reverse the pattern. The row of straight gobelin (3-ply yarn) appears on both charts; work only one row. Miter the corners. Work border stitches (3-ply yarn) last so the yarn does not become fuzzy from handling.

For Border

Line Chart: horizontal and vertical grid lines represent horizontal and vertical lines on the canvas.

Work the border in the bargello stitch.

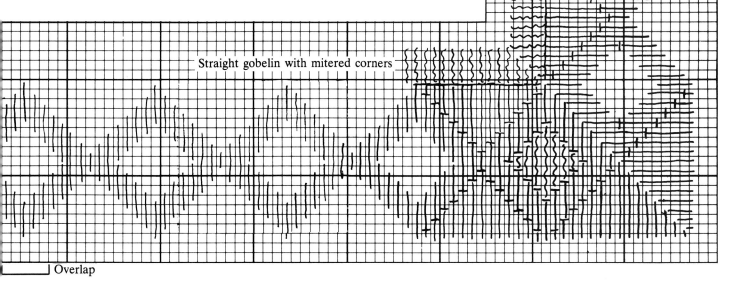

Straight gobelin with mitered corners

Overlap

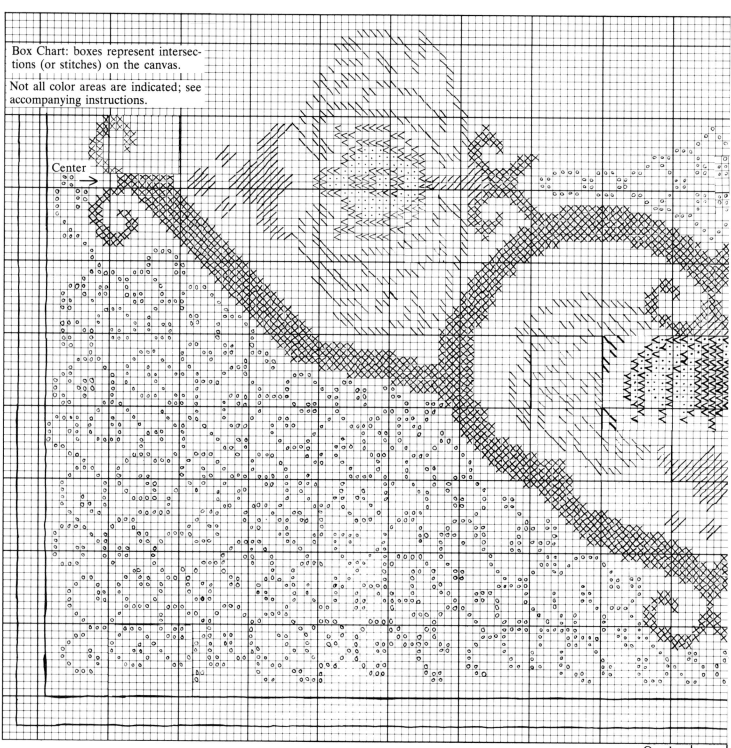

Box Chart: boxes represent intersections (or stitches) on the canvas.

Not all color areas are indicated; see accompanying instructions.

Center

Overlap

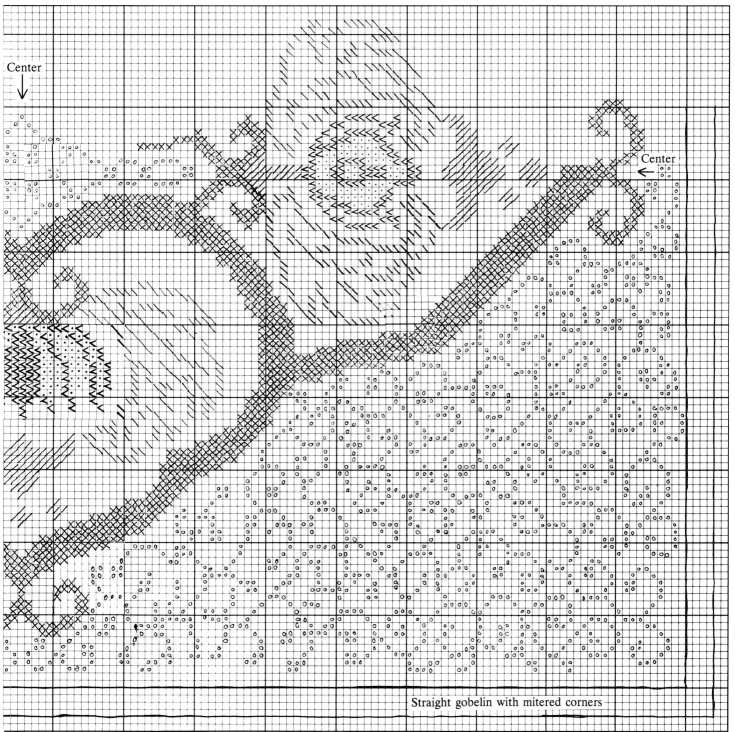

Center

Center

Straight gobelin with mitered corners

Overlap

PEONIES
IN SPRING

One of the more elegant of the designs, this motif was copied from an antique Chinese dish. The design, which appears so complicated in its entirety, becomes manageable when it is marked by sections. The two charts that combine to make the total design are carefully marked at the centers so they can be matched. Some colors are not indicated on the chart; see the instructions below for filling in some of the color areas.

Canvas Size: 25″ × 20″ piece of #13 white canvas

Finished Size: 21″ × 16″ if worked on #13 canvas

Chart Thread Count: 270 wide × 207 high

Color Code (Paterna):
- ◩ green (526)
- ■ dark blue (334)
- □ dark blue (334) in sections of border design
- ◪ medium blue (385)
- ⊡ dark gold (433)
- ⊠ medium gold (445)
- □ medium gold (445) in flower on the right side of the main design
- ◩ light gold (453)
- □ light gold (453) in flower at top left of central design and in leaves
- ⊙ rust (215)
- □ rust (215) in sections of border design
- □ cream (040) in background of main design and parts of border design

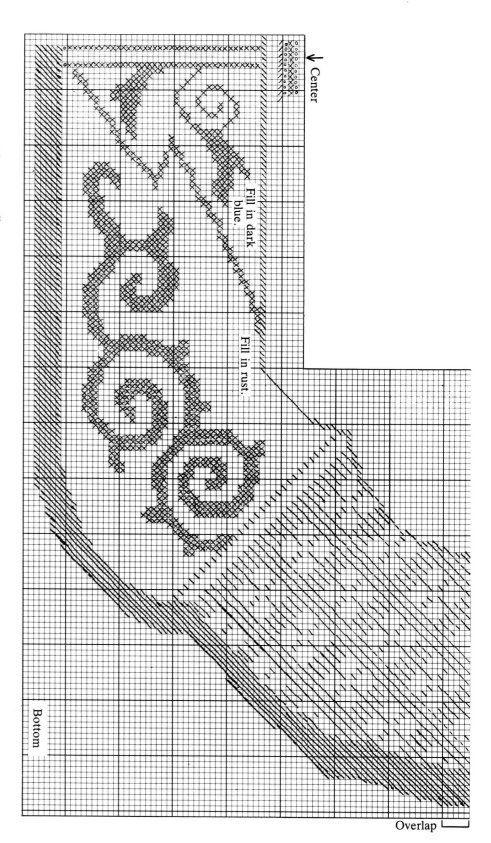

Overlap

Stitches: continental, basket-weave, and diagonal mosaic

Instructions:

Note: The chart for the central design area appears on page 84.

Find the center of your canvas as described on page 15.

Matching the center of the chart and the center of your canvas, mark the major design area as explained on page 15. Match the center markings for the two charts and continue marking the canvas for the border area.

Mark the top of the canvas so you remember to work basketweave without turning the canvas, thus insuring that all stitches slant from lower left to upper right. With the exception of the two large flowers, the entire design with border is worked in continental and bas-

ketweave (2-ply yarn). Use continental for outlines and single rows of stitches and basketweave for larger areas.

Work the marked areas within the central design area.

Fill in the unmarked areas of the leaves with light gold.

Fill in the large flower at the top left of the design with light gold using the diagonal mosaic stitch (2-ply yarn) from the Portfolio of Stitches, page 25.

Fill in the large flower on the right side of the design with medium gold in the diagonal mosaic stitch (2-ply yarn).

Work the marked areas in the border. Fill in the blue and rust sections of the background as directed on the chart. Fill in the remainder of the background with cream.

Box Chart: boxes represent intersections (or stitches) on the canvas.

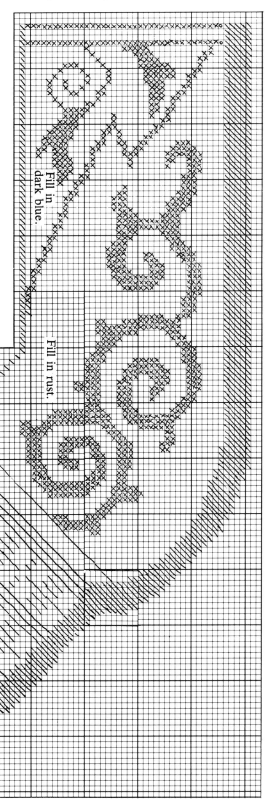

Overlap

Box Chart: boxes represent intersections (or stitches) on the canvas.

Not all color areas are indicated; see accompanying instructions.

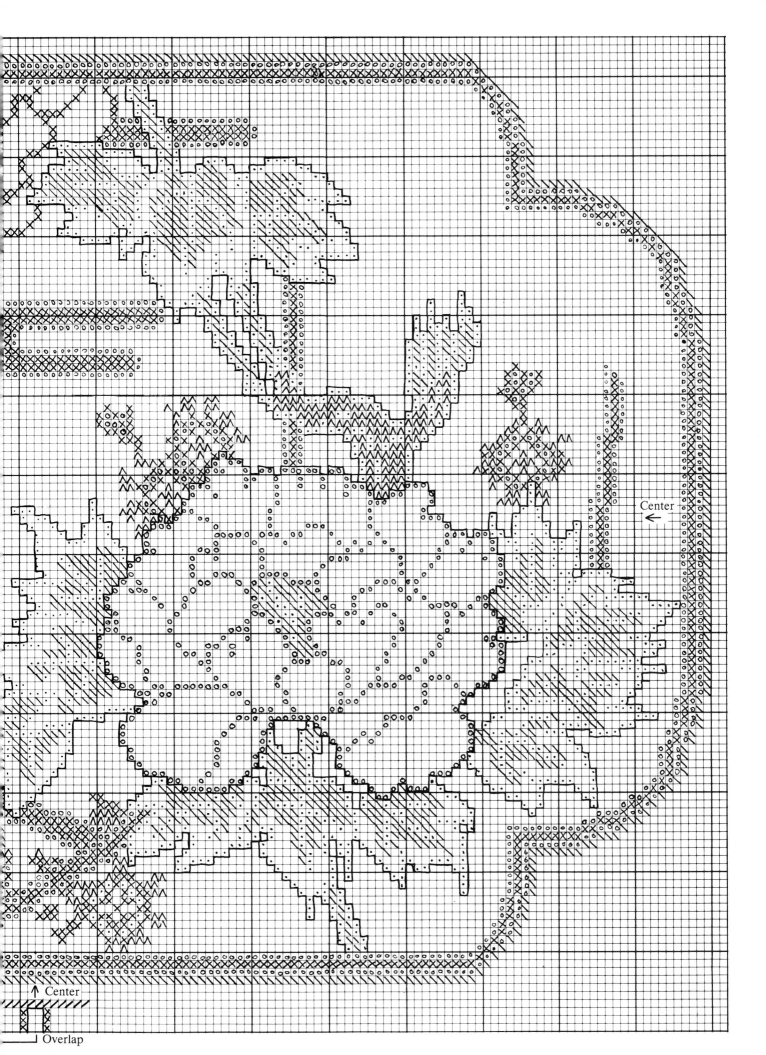

Center
←

↑ Center

⌐⌐ Overlap

CHINESE FERTILITY SYMBOL

To the Chinese, this motif of a pair of fish symbolizes marriage and fertility and is a charm against evil. Not all areas are marked for color; read the instructions below for additional color areas and for changes of stitches within the design.

Canvas Size: 21″ × 21″ piece of #13 white canvas

Finished Size: 17″ × 17″ if worked on #13 canvas

Chart Thread Count: 226 wide × 226 high

Color Code (Paterna):
- ▨ dark blue (334)
- ⊙ medium blue (385)
- ⊠ light blue (395)
- ☐ light blue (395) in background
- ⊡ cream (040)
- ■ dark gold (433)
- ☐ dark gold (433) in row of straight gobelin
- ◺ medium gold (445)
- ☐ medium gold (445) in row of straight gobelin
- ☐ light gold (453) inside fish

Stitches: continental, basketweave, diagonal mosaic, straight gobelin with mitered corners, and bargello

Instructions:

Find the center of your canvas as described on page 15.

Beginning with the center of the design, mark your canvas as explained on page 15.

Mark the top of the canvas so you remember to work basketweave without turning the canvas, thus insuring that all stitches slant from lower left to upper right.

Work all of the marked areas except the tails of the fish in continental and basketweave (2-ply yarn), using continental for outlines and single rows of stitches and basketweave for larger areas.

Work the outline of the tails in continental. Fill in the remaining marked areas of the tails with diagonal mosaic (2-ply yarn).

Work the unmarked area of the tails and fins in light gold with diagonal mosaic.

Fill in all other unmarked areas of the fish in light gold with continental or basketweave.

Work the background area in light blue with diagonal mosaic.

The design area is surrounded by a combination of two rows of straight gobelin and a bargello border. Allow 4 threads of canvas for each row of straight gobelin (total of 8 threads) between the design area and the border area. Before working the straight gobelin, work the bargello border (Border #1) shown on page 116.

Then work the rows of straight gobelin (3-ply yarn); miter the corners. Do the inside row of straight gobelin in dark gold and the outside row in medium gold.

Box Chart: boxes represent intersections (or stitches) on the canvas.

Not all color areas are indicated; see accompanying instructions.

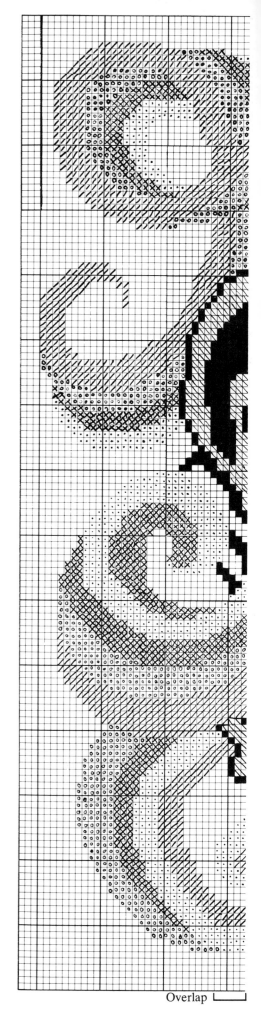

Overlap

Center
←

FOO LION

The lion, Chinese symbol of valor and power, is the focus of this pattern of blues on cream. The lion in basketweave contrasts with the clouds in diagonal mosaic. A striking bargello border and row of straight gobelin in colors that repeat those of the lion frame the central motif.

Canvas Size: 21″ × 17″ piece of #13 white canvas

Finished Size (including bargello border): 17″ × 13″ if worked on #13 canvas.

Chart Thread Count: 220 wide × 166 high

Color Code (Paterna):

◩ dark blue (334)
☐ dark blue (334) in unmarked area of ball of yarn and in row of straight gobelin
◉ medium blue (385)
☐ light blue (395) in unmarked area of clouds
☐ cream (040) in unmarked area of lion and background

Stitches: continental, basketweave, diagonal mosaic, straight gobelin with mitered corners, and bargello

Instructions:

Find the center of your canvas as described on page 15.

Beginning with the center of the design, mark your canvas as explained on page 15.

Mark the top of your canvas to remind yourself to work all basketweave without turning the canvas, thus insuring that all stitches slant from lower left to upper right. The straight gobelin and bargello border are worked from four directions.

Use continental and basketweave (2-ply yarn) in all the area of the central design. Use continental for outlines and single rows of stitches and basketweave for larger areas.

Work the marked areas of the design.

Fill in the remainder of the ball of yarn with dark blue in the diagonal mosaic (2-ply yarn).

Fill in the cloud areas with light blue in the diagonal mosaic (2-ply yarn).

The remainder of the design and background is worked with cream in continental and basketweave (2-ply yarn).

Allow 4 threads of canvas for working a row of straight gobelin between the design area and the bargello border.

Before working the straight gobelin, work the bargello border that appears on page 116.

Work the straight gobelin (3-ply yarn) in dark blue; miter the corners. This is worked last because it may become fuzzy if handled too much.

Work a row of straight gobelin with mitered corners around the outside edge of the pillow.

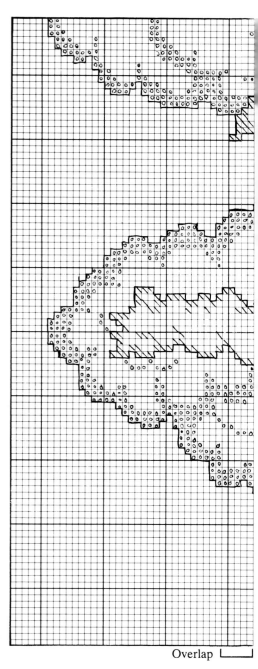

Overlap

Box Chart: boxes represent intersections (or stitches) on the canvas.

Not all color areas are indicated; see accompanying instructions.

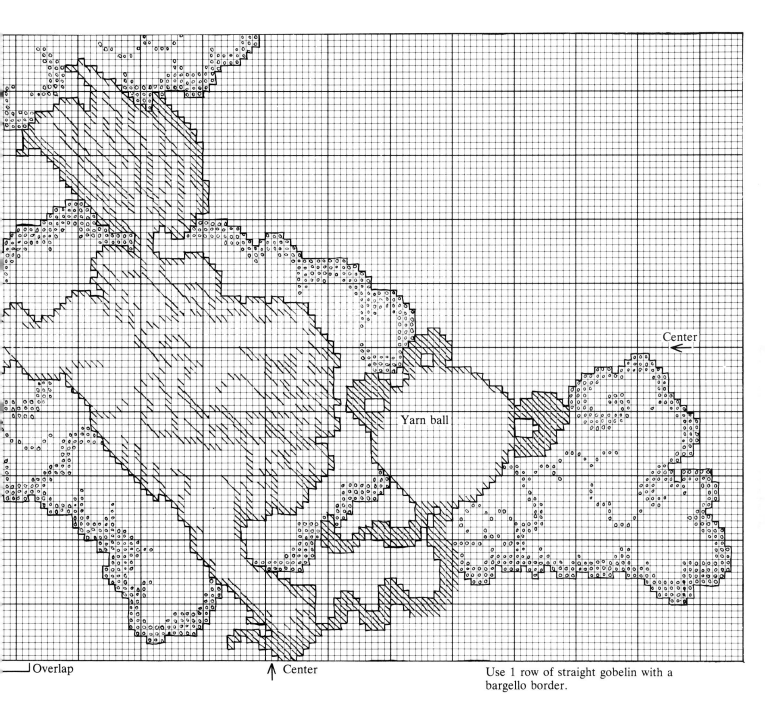

Yarn ball

Center ←

┘ Overlap   ↑ Center   Use 1 row of straight gobelin with a
                                     bargello border.

BLACK & WHITE SHELLS

Seashells in basketweave are set against sand and coral in textured stitches within the frame of a row of straight gobelin and a bargello border. To simplify the chart, not all the design areas are marked.

Symbols on the chart may represent either colors or stitches. The colors shown in the photograph are black, medium gray, light gray, and white. The design can be worked in shades of any color. Worked in blues, this design makes a striking companion to the Blue Shells.

Follow the instructions below to combine stitches and colors within the design area.

Canvas Size: 20″ × 17″ piece of #13 white canvas

Finished Size (including bargello border): 16″ × 13″ if worked on #13 canvas

Chart Thread Count: 204 wide × 172 high

Color Code (Paterna):
- ⊡ black (050)
- ⊠ medium gray (162)
- ☐ light gray (166) in unmarked areas inside shells and in smyrna cross stitches in coral design area
- ☐ white (012) in background and in smyrna cross and double leviathan stitches in sand area

Stitches: continental, basketweave, smyrna cross (indicated by ⊠), double leviathan (indicated by ⊠), straight gobelin with mitered corners, and bargello

Instructions:

Find the center of your canvas as described on page 15.

Beginning with the center of the design, mark the canvas as explained on page 15, being careful to distinguish between the symbols for color and for stitches.

Mark the top of your canvas so you remember to work basketweave without turning the canvas, thus insuring that the stitches slant from lower left to upper right. The bargello border will be worked from four directions.

Work the shell motifs, the outline of the coral design, and the background in continental and basketweave (2-ply yarn), using continental for outlines and single rows of stitches and basketweave for larger areas.

Fill in the unmarked area inside the shells with the light gray yarn. Work the smyrna cross stitches that are part of the coral design in light gray (2-ply yarn). Work the smyrna cross and double leviathan stitches that make up the sand area in white (2-ply yarn).

Allow 4 threads of canvas for working the row of straight gobelin between the central design and the border. Before working the straight gobelin, work the bargello border (Border #3) that appears on page 120. Then work the straight gobelin (3-ply yarn) in black; miter the corners of the framing row of straight gobelin.

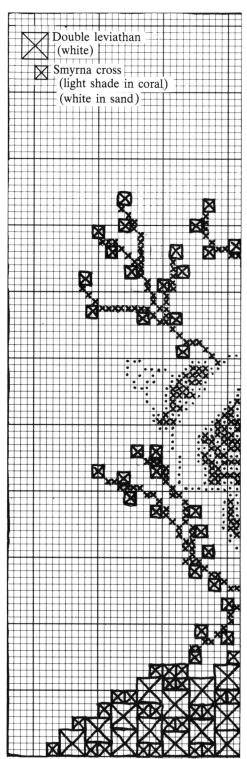

Double leviathan (white)

Smyrna cross (light shade in coral) (white in sand)

Overlap

Center
↓

← Center

└─┘ Overlap   Use 1 row of straight gobelin with a bargello border.

Box Chart: boxes represent intersections (or stitches) on the canvas.

Symbols on this chart may represent color or stitch; see accompanying instructions.

BLUE SHELLS

Texturally exciting, this design appears complex because some of the symbols on the chart indicate color and others indicate the stitch to use. Read the instructions below carefully and you will have no difficulty in distinguishing between the two types of symbols.

Canvas Size: 15″ × 15″ piece of #13 white canvas

Finished Size (including bargello border): 11″ × 11″ if worked on #13 canvas

Chart Thread Count: 148 wide × 140 high

Color Code (Paterna):
- ◹ dark blue (334)
- ⊠ medium blue (385)
- ⊡ light blue (395)
- ☐ light blue (395) for working smyrna cross stitches in coral design area
- ☐ cream (040) for background and for smyrna cross and double leviathan stitches in sand area

Stitches: continental, basketweave, smyrna cross (indicated by ⊠), double leviathan (indicated by ⊠), and bargello

Instructions:

Find the center of your canvas as described on page 15.

Beginning with the center of the design, mark the canvas as explained on page 15, being careful to distinguish between the symbols for color and those for stitches.

Mark the top of your canvas so you remember to work basketweave without turning the canvas, thus insuring that the stitches slant from lower left to upper right. The bargello border will be worked in four directions.

The shell, the outline for the coral, and the background are all worked in continental and basketweave (2-ply yarn), using continental for outlines and single rows of stitches and basketweave for larger areas.

Work the smyrna cross stitches that are a part of the coral design area in light blue (2-ply yarn). Work the smyrna cross and double leviathan stitches in the sand design area in cream (2-ply yarn).

The bargello border shown with this pillow appears on page 116. Notice that the color code for the border is different from the color code for this central design.

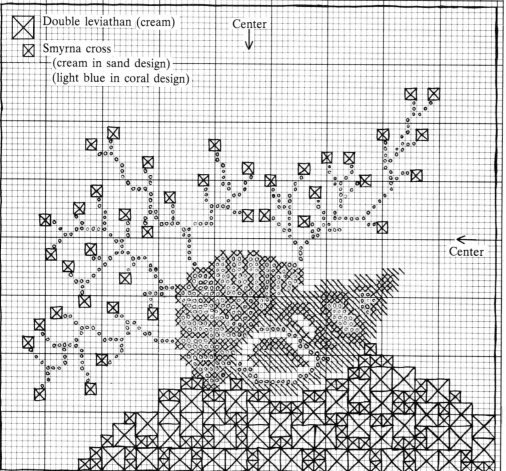

Double leviathan (cream)

Smyrna cross (cream in sand design) (light blue in coral design)

Center

Center

Box Chart: boxes represent intersections (or stitches) on the canvas.

Symbols on this chart may represent color or stitch; see accompanying instructions.

Opposite Above: Square Sampler, chart on page 100.

Opposite Below: Four-Way Stitches, chart on page 106.

Rectangular Sampler, chart on page 102.

KALEIDOSCOPE

A moment in the turning of a kaleidoscope is captured in this design with its repeated images against a textured background. If you are not accustomed to matching different stitches, this will present a new challenge for you, for the design requires many compensating stitches. Read the instructions below for information on changing stitches.

Canvas Size: 18″ × 18″ piece of #13 white canvas

Finished Size: 14″ × 14″ if worked on #13 canvas

Chart Thread Count: 178 wide × 178 high

Color Code (Paterna):
- ■ dark blue (334)
- □ dark blue (334) used in border stitch around central design
- ☒ medium blue (385)
- ⊡ light blue (395)
- ◫ medium gold (445)
- □ cream (040) used in background

Eight-Way Stitches, chart on page 107.

Stitches: continental, basketweave, brick, and diamond cross

Instructions:

Note: The Kaleidoscope chart appears on the following page.

Find the center of your canvas as described on page 15.

Beginning with the center of the design, mark your canvas as described on page 15. You have been given more than one-fourth of the design. Turn the canvas to complete the pattern, being careful to match the pattern at the center. Do not repeat the center lines. Refer to the photograph on page 35 for help with placing the pattern.

Mark the top of your canvas so you remember to work basketweave without turning the canvas, thus insuring that all stitches slant from lower left to upper right. Work the area within the border line in continental and basketweave (2-ply yarn), using continental for outlines and single rows of stitches and basketweave for larger areas.

Work the border line of Pattern 1 of the brick stitch in dark blue over 4 threads of canvas (3-ply yarn). Work so that the needle goes into the worked area from the top of the canvas. These stitches are worked from the four sides of the canvas and are mitered where the sections meet.

Work the diamond cross stitch (2-ply yarn) in rows to fill the background area. Be sure this stitch goes into the same hole of the canvas as that used by the outer edge of the brick stitch. The diamond cross stitch requires more yarn than most stitches so be sure to allow for this when you purchase yarn.

Keep the rows in a straight pattern. Compensating stitches may be necessary to fill in next to the blue outline border. To do this, simply work as much of the stitch as you have room for on the canvas.

This design can be varied by filling in the area beyond the border line with more basketweave in cream or by changing the color of the area worked in diamond cross stitch.

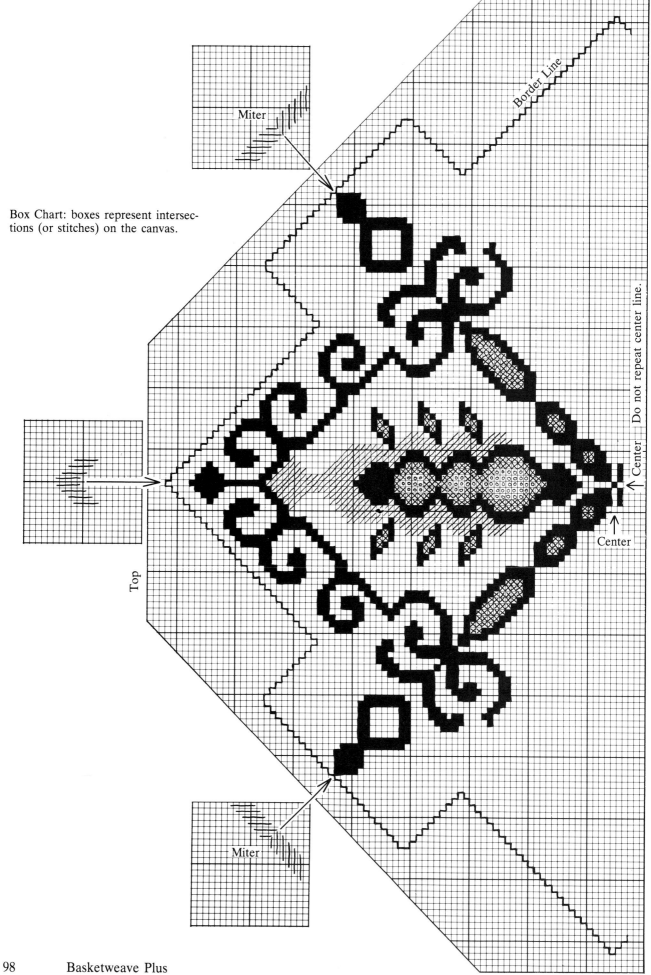

Box Chart: boxes represent intersections (or stitches) on the canvas.

Miter

Border Line

Center — Do not repeat center line.

Center

Top

Miter

Multiple Stitches

The four designs in this section are used in my shop as "sampler" designs on which students practice working decorative stitches. Square Sampler and Rectangular Sampler are used for beginners, and Four-Way Stitches and Eight-Way Stitches are used for my more advanced students. Each design has many kinds of stitches but not many of each kind; this keeps you from tiring of one you might not like.

Each of the first three designs has a center portion that is counted from a chart. Around this charted and counted area, rows of stitches are used to make borders. Each of the stitches in the border areas is diagrammed and defined in the Portfolio of Stitches, page 21. Except for the combination of a rhodes stitch and shell stitches worked over 6 threads of canvas, the rows of stitches that make up the borders are each worked over 4 threads of canvas and can be interchanged to suit your wishes. End each border area with a row of straight gobelin with mitered corners. This stitch gives a finished, almost framed, appearance to the pillow.

All four charts in this chapter are line charts—the horizontal and vertical lines of the grid represent horizontal and vertical threads on the canvas. Since there are no color differences in three of the designs, stitches are drawn onto the chart exactly as they will look

on your canvas. In the Eight-Way Stitches design, the stitches drawn on the chart are worked in one color and the background is worked in a contrasting color.

Brown canvas works well with decorative stitch designs because it is less noticeable between stitches. (The Eight-Way Stitches design, however, should be worked on white canvas because part of the design can be marked and is easier to follow on white canvas.)

An interesting feature of these pillows is that there is no "right side up"—the designs seem to radiate from the center. The instructions accompanying each design explain how changes of directions are to be worked.

Each design is easily modified. The combinations of rows of stitches used in the border areas may be rearranged. The pillows may be worked in a single shade of light or medium colored yarn or in any combination of colors. (Dark shades do not work well.) The Eight-Way Stitches design could be worked in light and medium shades of any color.

Chart thread counts are not given with three of the charts. Do not change mesh size. The combination of 3-ply yarn and #13 canvas is needed for some of the decorative stitches of these designs. If you change to a larger canvas mesh, some of the stitches may leave canvas showing.

SQUARE SAMPLER

The center section of this pillow design consists of a 6″ square; that is the only portion of the design that is charted. The remainder of the design is made up of rows of various stitches that can be worked over 4 or 6 threads of canvas. Each of the stitches is diagrammed in the Portfolio of Stitches, page 21. Only one color of yarn is used. The complexity of the design is a result of the use of many stitches. It is easy to vary the size of this pillow by adding or subtracting rows of stitches, but be sure to allow extra canvas if you increase size.

Canvas Size: 18″ × 18″ piece of #13 brown canvas

Finished Size: 14″ × 14″ if worked on #13 canvas

Color (Paterna):
off-white (012) or any light or medium shade of yarn

Stitches: brick, leaf, basketweave, rhodes, shell, straight gobelin with mitered corners, crossed corners, scotch, and double leviathan

Instructions:
Find the center of your canvas as described on page 15.

Beginning in the center of your canvas, count down 42 threads and then count 42 threads to the right. This is the lower right corner of the chart.

Work the main outlines of the design with 3-ply yarn. The resulting configuration should resemble the diagram.

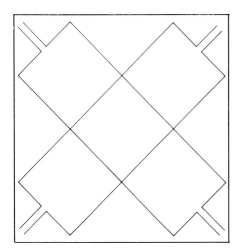

Fill in all the pyramid areas of the chart, using 3-ply yarn.

Notice that between the sections of worked area you have 2 threads of empty canvas. Using 2-ply yarn, fill in completely with Pattern 1 of the brick stitch.

In the center square there are four dots that indicate where the tops of the large leaf stitches start. Work the four leaf stitches with 2-ply yarn.

In the four remaining squares, work the stitches so that they point toward the center square. Turn the chart so the square you are working is in the same position on the chart as it is on your canvas. Work the lines in the squares with 3-ply yarn. Bring the needle up in the hole marked with

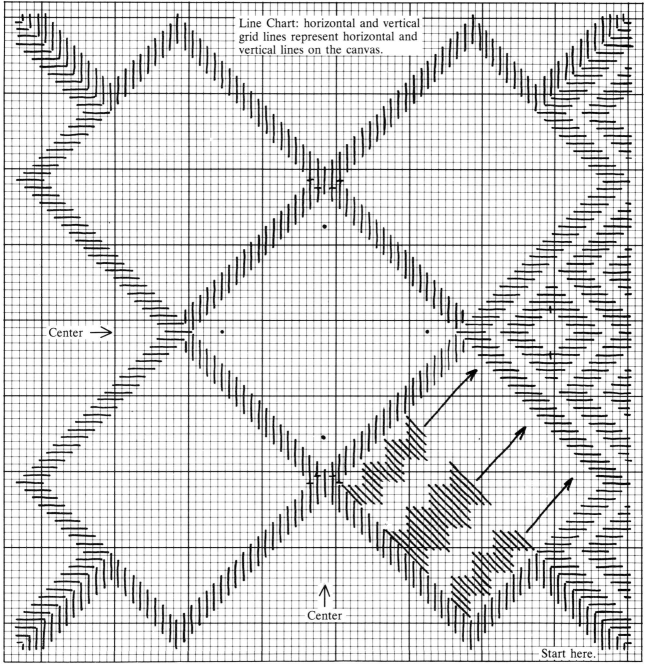

Line Chart: horizontal and vertical grid lines represent horizontal and vertical lines on the canvas.

Center →

Center ↑

Start here.

a dot in the box. Work the first row of stitches from center toward the left. Reverse the pattern and finish the row by working toward the right. Work the other two rows by starting in the center and working left, then starting again in the center and working right.

Use the basketweave stitch, with 2-ply yarn, to fill in the remaining areas of the central design. To determine the direction of the basketweave, hold the pillow so the lines of the center of the leaf motif make a cross (+). Extend these lines in your imagination so that they divide the design into quadrants. Beginning in the upper right quadrant, work the basketweave as you normally would so that the stitches slant from lower left to upper right. When you have completed this fourth of the design, turn the canvas 90 degrees. Again, work the upper right quadrant as you did the first. Continue until the basketweave is complete in all four quadrants.

Using the photograph on page 93 as a guide to placement, work a rhodes stitch (2-ply yarn) over 6 threads of canvas at each corner of the central design.

Between the rhodes stitches on each corner, work the shell stitch over 6 threads using 2-ply yarn.

The remaining eleven border rows are worked over 4 threads of canvas. Alter the order as desired, but end with a straight gobelin to give a finished, or framed, look to the pillow. The order that follows is the one used on the pillow in the photograph:

Straight gobelin with 3-ply yarn. Miter the corners.

Crossed corners with 2-ply yarn.

Straight gobelin with 3-ply yarn. Miter the corners.

Two rows of scotch stitch with 2-ply yarn.

Straight gobelin with 3-ply yarn. Miter the corners.

Double leviathan with 2-ply yarn.

Straight gobelin with 3-ply yarn. Miter the corners.

Two rows of scotch stitch with 2-ply yarn.

Straight gobelin with 3-ply yarn. Miter the corners.

RECTANGULAR SAMPLER

A rectangular sampler pillow is made up of a central area with stitches counted from a chart and a series of border rows of decorative stitches. Although a single shade of yarn is used here, the beauty of the design is produced through the use of the various stitches. Each of the stitches is diagrammed in the Portfolio of Stitches, page 21. Add or subtract rows of stitches to make a pillow the size you want, but allow extra canvas for a larger pillow.

Canvas Size: 23″ × 15″ piece of #13 brown canvas

Finished Size: 19″ × 11″ if worked on #13 canvas

Color (Paterna):
light gold (492) or any light or medium shade of yarn

Stitches: brick, leaf, basketweave, rhodes, shell, straight gobelin with mitered corners, crossed corners, and scotch

Instructions:
Note: All four charts for the rectangular sampler appear on pages 104-105.

Find the center of your canvas as described on page 15.

To find the starting point on your canvas, count down from the center 42 threads and to the right 74 threads. This corresponds to the point marked in the lower right of the chart.

Work the stitches indicated on Chart A with 3-ply yarn.

Notice that Chart B repeats the lines of stitches that you have already worked from Chart A. This chart adds the stitches in the pyramids around the outer edges of the design. Work these pyramids in 3-ply yarn as they are shown on Chart B. The chart gives the pyramids for the full dimension of the short sides of the design but only half the long side. Reverse the pattern to complete the long sides.

When you have worked the lines for Chart B, you will see that there are two empty threads of canvas between the sections of worked area. Fill in these empty areas of all the pyramids (2-ply yarn) with Pattern 1 of the brick stitch.

Chart C repeats some main lines from Chart A. Use 3-ply yarn to add the new lines from Chart C, turning the chart to work the second half of the design. Be sure to work the lines within the four outer squares (labelled box D) so that the stitches slant toward the center of the design. Refer to Chart D to check the direction of the lines.

Dots on Chart C indicate the placement for the tops of large leaf stitches. Work these

stitches with 2-ply yarn. Where four leaves meet to make a pinwheel, extend the side sections until the center hole is used.

Fill in the remaining areas of the four outermost squares and the squares containing the pinwheels with basketweave worked with 2-ply yarn in the directions indicated on the diagram. To work each section, turn the diagram and the canvas so the arrow for that section points from lower left to upper right. Holding the canvas in that position, work one section. Then turn your canvas as needed to work the other sections in Figure 1.

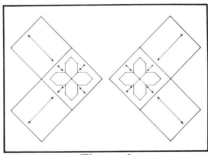

Figure 1

The remainder of the design area is filled with Pattern 2 of the brick stitch. Use 2-ply yarn. Work the brick stitch in the direction indicated by the arrows of Figure 2.

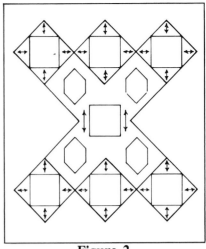

Figure 2

Using the photograph on page 94 as a guide, work a rhodes stitch (2-ply yarn) over 6 threads of canvas at each corner of the central design. Between the rhodes stitches at the corners, work a row of shell stitch (2-ply yarn) over 6 threads of canvas. On both long sides of the pillow, make the last shell stitch with five uprights instead of the usual four so the border will fit.

The remaining border rows are worked over 4 threads of canvas in the following sequence, although you may alter the order as you wish so long as each row of the stitches is worked over 4 threads of canvas.

Straight gobelin with 3-ply yarn. Miter the corners.

Crossed corners with 2-ply yarn.

Straight gobelin with 3-ply yarn. Miter the corners.

Two rows of scotch stitch with 2-ply yarn.

Line Chart: horizontal and vertical
grid lines represent horizontal and
vertical lines on the canvas.

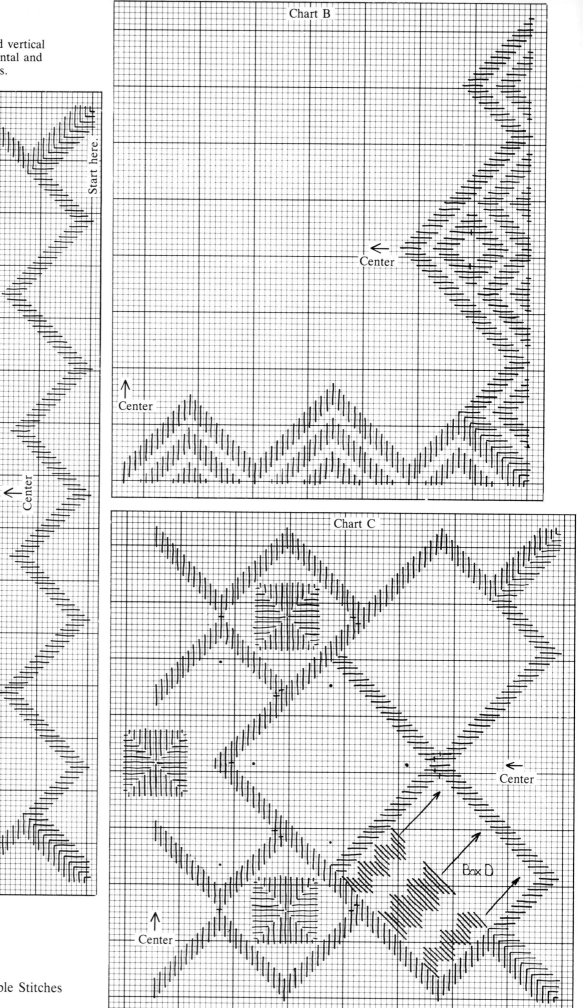

Chart B

Center

Center

Chart C

Center

Box D

Center

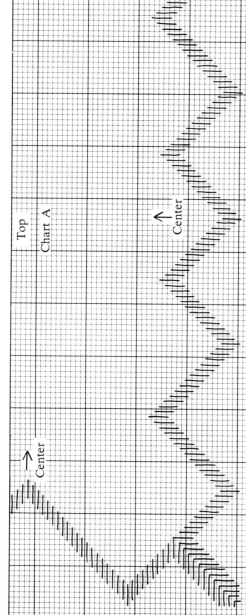

Top

Chart A

Center

Center

Start here.

Chart D

FOUR-WAY STITCHES

Like most of the designs in this chapter, this design of decorative stitches is worked in only one color to emphasize the complexity of the individual stitches. The design is composed of a square that is worked from a chart and surrounded by a border of rows of decorative stitches. Each of the stitches is diagrammed in the Portfolio of Stitches, page 21. The central design is worked from the center with the quarters worked separately. To vary the size of the design, vary the number of rows of decorative stitches. For a larger pillow, allow extra canvas.

Canvas Size: 20″ × 20″ piece of #13 brown canvas

Line Chart: horizontal and vertical grid lines represent horizontal and vertical lines on the canvas.

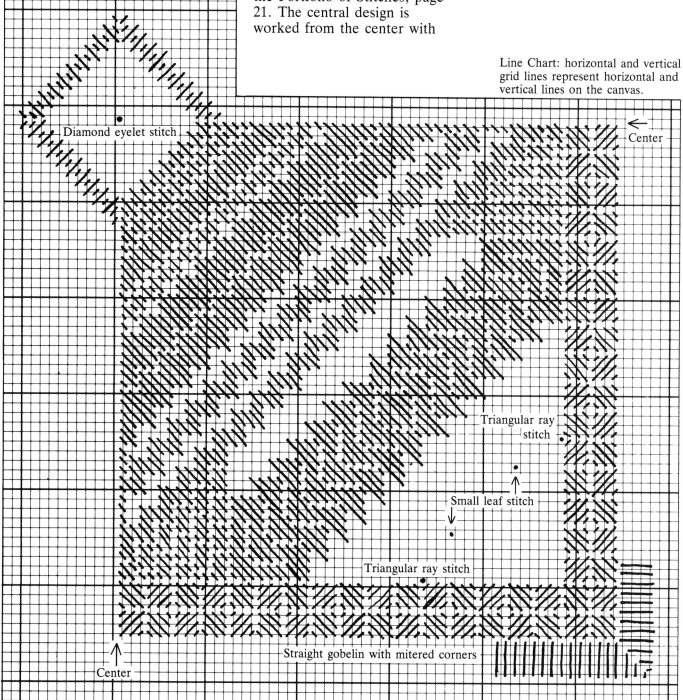

Finished Size: 13″ × 13″ if worked on #13 canvas

Color (Paterna):
off-white (012) or any light or medium shade of yarn

Stitches: triangular ray, diamond eyelet, small leaf, scotch, straight gobelin with mitered corners, basketweave, crossed corners, double leviathan, large cross/straight cross, shell, and rhodes

Instructions:

Find the center of your canvas as described on page 15.

Beginning with the central design, work outward to complete each quarter. Everything on the chart is worked with 2-ply yarn except the straight gobelin that is worked with 3-ply. Dots are marked to indicate the centers of triangular ray and diamond eyelet stitches. Dots also indicate the tops, or points, of small leaf stitches.

After all the stitches indicated on the chart are worked, fill in the remaining area of the center design with basketweave that slants in the direction of the other stitches. Working by fourths of the design, work each top right quadrant with the basketweave stitches slanting from lower left to upper right. Rotate your canvas and continue working by quadrants. (See diagram.)

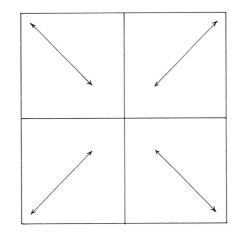

The six rows of border stitches beyond the straight gobelin, which is shown on the chart, can be chosen from the Portfolio of Stitches, page 21. To complete the pillow to the finished size of 13″ × 13″, work five of the remaining rows over 4 threads; work one over 6 threads. End with a row of straight gobelin.

The stitches used to make the sequence of rows shown in the photograph on page 93 include these:

Crossed corners with 2-ply yarn.

Double leviathan with 2-ply yarn.

Large cross/straight cross stitch with 2-ply yarn.

Straight gobelin with 3-ply yarn. Miter the corners.

Shell stitches with rhodes stitches at corners (worked over 6 threads of canvas) with 2-ply yarn.

Straight gobelin with 3-ply yarn. Miter the corners.

EIGHT-WAY STITCHES

The stitches in this design are worked in eight different directions. To make this design more manageable, mark the single stitches in light green. This establishes the basic design and turns the puzzler into an easier project.

Canvas Size: 14″ × 14″ piece of #13 white canvas

Finished Size: 10″ × 10″ if worked on #13 canvas

Colors (Paterna):
light green (593) for all marks on chart
medium green (553) in background

Stitches: leaf and basketweave

Instructions:

Note: The chart for this design appears on the next page.

Find the center of your canvas as described on page 15.

The chart shows one-half the design. Match the center of the chart to the center of your canvas; when half has been marked, rotate the chart to line up on the center line. Do not repeat the center line.

Mark as explained on page 15 and work all the single stitches (2-ply yarn) that show on the chart, slanting the stitches as they are drawn on the chart.

Count and work the long, straight stitches drawn on the chart.

Work large leaf stitches between the dots on the chart. Refer to the photograph on page 96 for help with placement and direction. There are 4 single leaf stitches and 4 "pinwheels" consisting of 4 leaf stitches each. The centers of the 4 pinwheels are also indicated by a dot on the chart. In these pinwheels, leaves are worked with a common center and extending to the four outer dots.

The background is basket-weave (2-ply yarn) in a medium green. To determine the direction of the background stitches in each section, imagine the lines along the centers of the leaf stitches dividing the canvas into fourths as shown in the diagram. Work the basket-weave background one-fourth at a time. Begin with Section A in the lower right corner of the canvas. Work with the stitch slanting from lower left to upper right. Rotate the canvas in a counter-clockwise direction so Section B is located in the lower right. Position and work the stitches as indicated. Continue this process with Sections C and D.

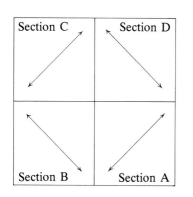

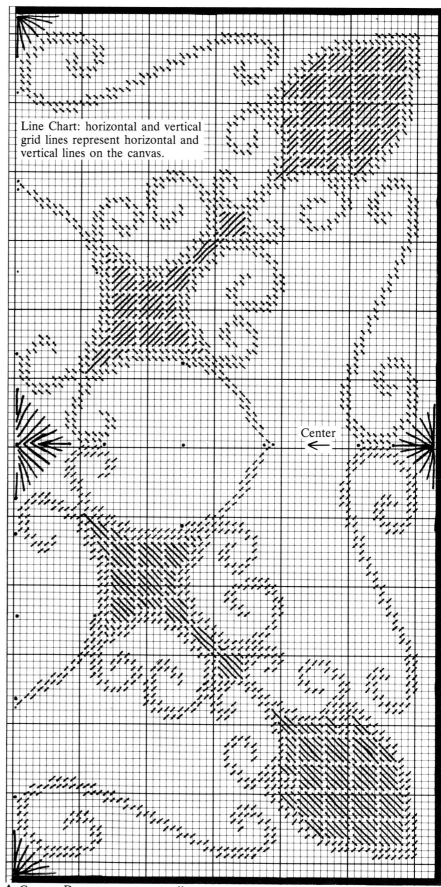

Line Chart: horizontal and vertical grid lines represent horizontal and vertical lines on the canvas.

Center

Center Do not repeat center line.

Bargello
& Borders

Bargello is a particularly pleasant form of needlepoint. Designs work up quickly because, with the longer stitches, it takes less time to cover the canvas. There seems to be no end to the geometric patterns that can be formed from these simple, straight stitches. The patterns appear to change even as you work because larger areas of the pattern give stronger impressions of complexity. The shades of colors in bargello create variations of depth that amount almost to optical illusion. A subtle change of one shade of color in a border will create a completely different pattern. Replace one shade with a contrasting color and you make the pattern almost unrecognizable.

The borders given here are color keyed in blues and cream or black, grays, and white to match certain designs that appear in other design chapters. If the colors of the central designs are changed, simply change the colors of the borders to match.

The length and pattern of the stitches in a row of bargello may vary, but the stitch always "wraps" the canvas. When the stitch follows the number sequence given with the diagram in the Portfolio of Stitches, page 37, the canvas will be wrapped and will not show through on a finished piece of needlepoint.

Chart thread counts are not given for bargello designs. Do not change mesh size, or you lose the balance between mesh size and yarn. I have found that #13 canvas and 3-ply yarn are the best combination for covering the canvas with bargello or with other decorative stitches.

STRAIGHT BARGELLO

In colors that mix easily with many of the other designs in this book, this bargello pillow works up quickly to provide a companion for other designs. Of course, it has enough pattern and textural interest so it could be used alone. The line charts have horizontal and vertical grid lines that represent horizontal and vertical lines of the canvas. The stitches drawn on the chart are to be worked in the bargello stitch. (See Portfolio of Stitches, page 37.) Remember that the bargello stitch wraps the canvas.

Canvas Size: 16½" × 16½" piece of #13 brown canvas

Finished Size: 12½" × 12½" if worked on #13 canvas

Colors (Paterna):
dark blue (334)
medium blue (385)
gold (445)
red (810)
cream (040)

Stitches: bargello

Instructions:
Use 3-ply yarn and brown canvas. Some people prefer to work bargello from a center line; others prefer to work from right to left beginning at the bottom of the design. Either way works well. The center line is marked for those who prefer to begin there. Or come in 2" from the right and bottom edges of your canvas to find the lower right corner of the design.

Work the main pattern in cream; colors for the rows between the main pattern rows are labelled on the chart. Work all of the main pattern, or combine the patterns as you work. The very short lines intersecting the stitch lines indicate the end of one stitch and the beginning of another stitch.

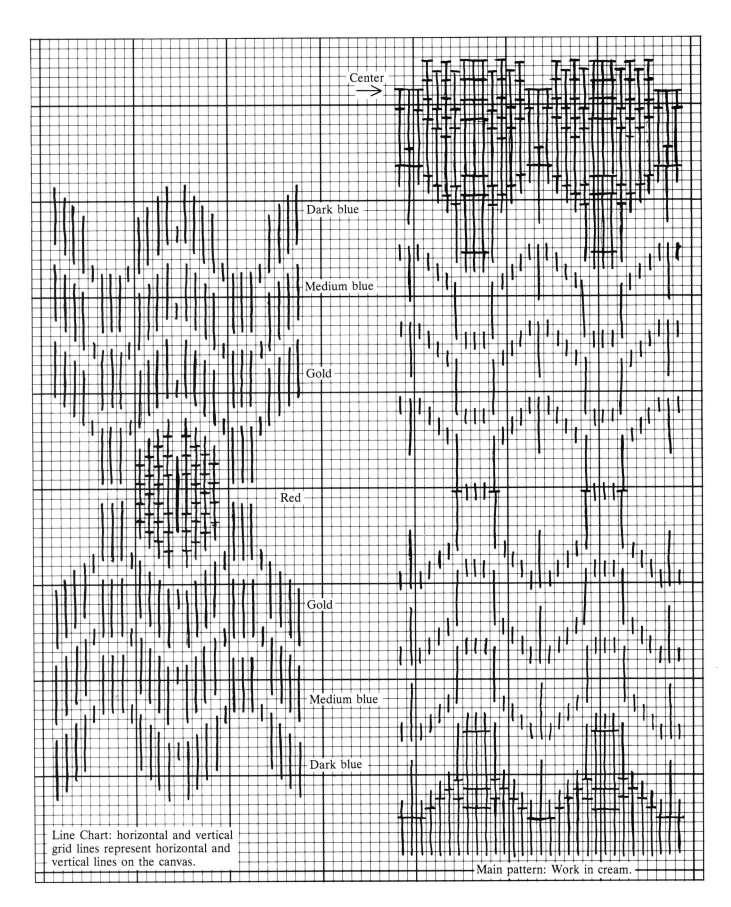

Center →

Dark blue

Medium blue

Gold

Red

Gold

Medium blue

Dark blue

Line Chart: horizontal and vertical grid lines represent horizontal and vertical lines on the canvas.

Main pattern: Work in cream.

FOUR-WAY BARGELLO

This design is worked from the four sides of the canvas and mitered at the corners. For more information on four-way bargello, refer to the Portfolio of Stitches, page 38.

Canvas Size: 17″ × 17″ piece of #13 brown canvas.

Finished Size: 13″ × 13″ if worked on #13 canvas

Colors (Paterna):
   dark blue (334)
   medium blue (385)
   gold (445)
   red (810)
   cream (040)

Stitches: four-way bargello

Instructions:

Use 3-ply yarn on brown canvas.

Divide your canvas along diagonal lines from corner to corner, using a single strand of yarn in a running stitch.

Some people prefer to work from the center outward, and others prefer to work from the outside edge to the center. Either method works well. Work the wavy lines in the center of the design in red. Work all other lines on the chart with cream, using the bargello stitch as described in the Portfolio of Stitches, page 37. The very short lines intersecting the stitch lines indicate the end of one stitch and the beginning of another.

Fill in between rows of cream with yarn in the colors on the chart, using a bargello stitch the length and pattern of the unmarked area of the canvas between rows.

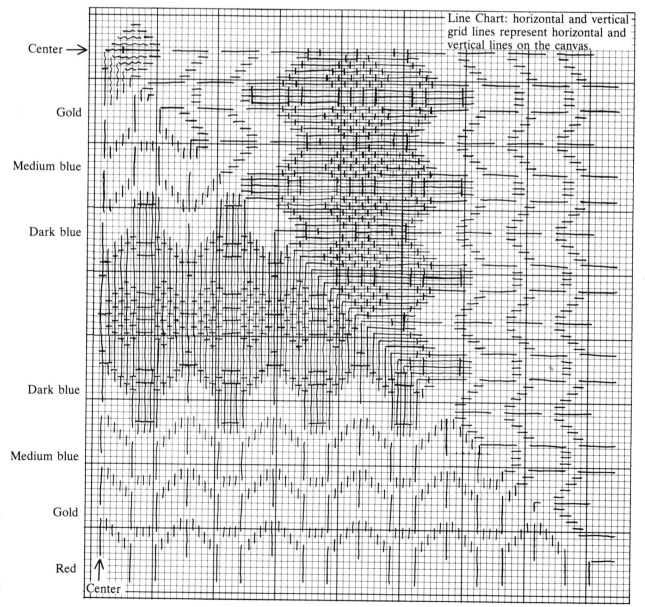

Center →

Gold

Medium blue

Dark blue

Dark blue

Medium blue

Gold

Red

↑ Center

Line Chart: horizontal and vertical grid lines represent horizontal and vertical lines on the canvas.

112

Four-Way Bargello, chart on page 112.

Straight Bargello, chart on page 110.

BARGELLO BORDERS

Bargello borders are the perfect frames for many of my designs. They are not as complex as they may appear.

Two charts are given for each border. The box chart (Chart A) gives the colors in which the stitches will be worked. The boxes on the charts represent the intersections of the canvas. The second chart (Chart B) is called a line chart and gives the length and placement of the stitches. Horizontal and vertical grid lines on this chart represent horizontal and vertical threads on the canvas. The two charts are used simultaneously in that you work the stitches shown on the line chart in the colors shown on the box chart.

Work the stitches on the line chart in the darkest shade shown on the color code. Fill in with the colors indicated on the box chart.

Remember that bargello is a "wrapping" stitch. Although the length and pattern of the bargello stitches may vary, the stitch always wraps the canvas. See the Portfolio of Stitches, page 37.

Always work borders after the central design area has been completed.

To insure that your border design is centered on each side, mark the corner diagonal lines and the center of each side with a strand of yarn as shown in the diagram. (Center marks are given on all charts for central designs.)

Begin stitching in one corner and work the pattern across the canvas until you reach the center mark for that side. Then reverse the pattern and work to the opposite miter line. Repeat the procedure for all four sides of the border. Miter the stitches at the corners of the borders into the diagonal rows of holes marked by the yarn.

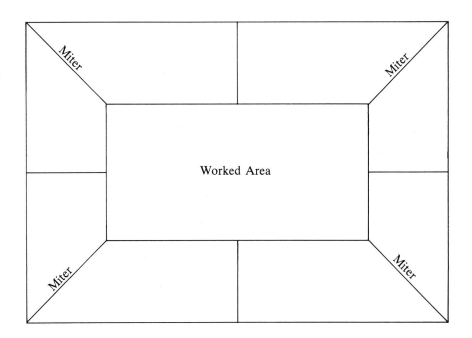

BORDER #1

This first pattern is the simplest to work and the simplest in its appearance. It is shown in the photographs of Foo Lion (page 88), Blue Shells (page 92), and the Chinese Fertility Symbol (page 86). It could also be used with Black & White Shells and Chinese Symbol for Success if you prefer it to the one shown with those designs.

The border is used sometimes with and sometimes without rows of straight gobelin between the design and the border.

The colors used in the borders are those that are used in the designs, but the color codes may differ. The border patterns could, of course, be worked in shades of other colors to go with different designs.

The design charts include allowances for enough canvas to work the border recommended for that design.

Color Code (Paterna):
⊠ dark blue (334)
◩ medium blue (385)
◙ light blue (395)
☐ cream (040)

Instructions:
Follow the general instructions for Bargello Borders, page 115.

Use 3-ply yarn.

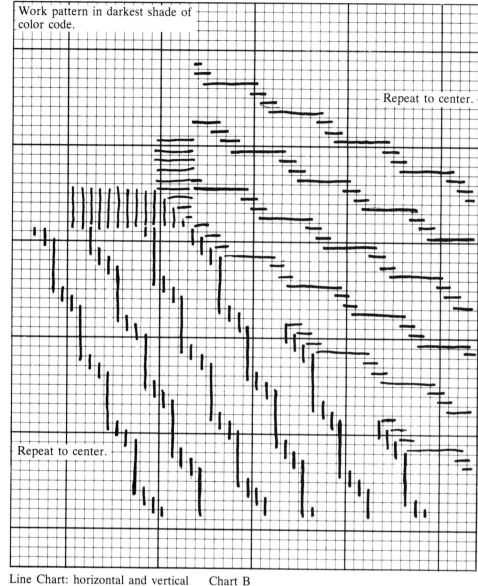

Work pattern in darkest shade of color code.

Repeat to center.

Repeat to center.

Chart B

Line Chart: horizontal and vertical grid lines represent horizontal and vertical lines on the canvas.

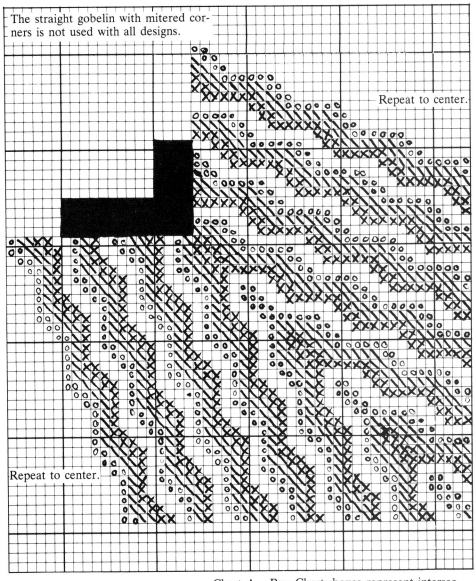

The straight gobelin with mitered corners is not used with all designs.

Repeat to center.

Repeat to center.

Chart A   Box Chart: boxes represent intersections (or stitches) on the canvas.

BORDER #2

Border #2 is used with Chinese Symbol for Success (page 66). The colors on the chart match the ones used in that central design.

The canvas allowance for the Symbol for Success includes an allowance for this border.

Color Code (Paterna):
⊠ dark blue (334)
⊡ medium blue (385)
⊠ light blue (395)
☐ cream (040)

Instructions:
Follow the general instructions for Bargello Borders, page 115.

Use 3-ply yarn.

Since the vertical and horizontal dimensions of Symbol for Success are different, the joining at the centers of the border will make a slightly different geometric design on vertical and horizontal sides of the pillow.

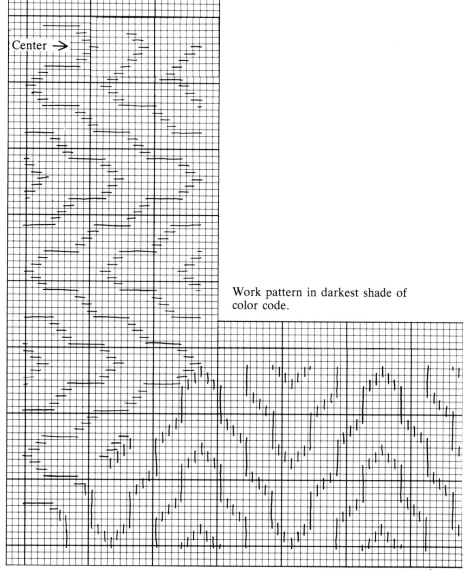

Center →

Work pattern in darkest shade of color code.

Overlap

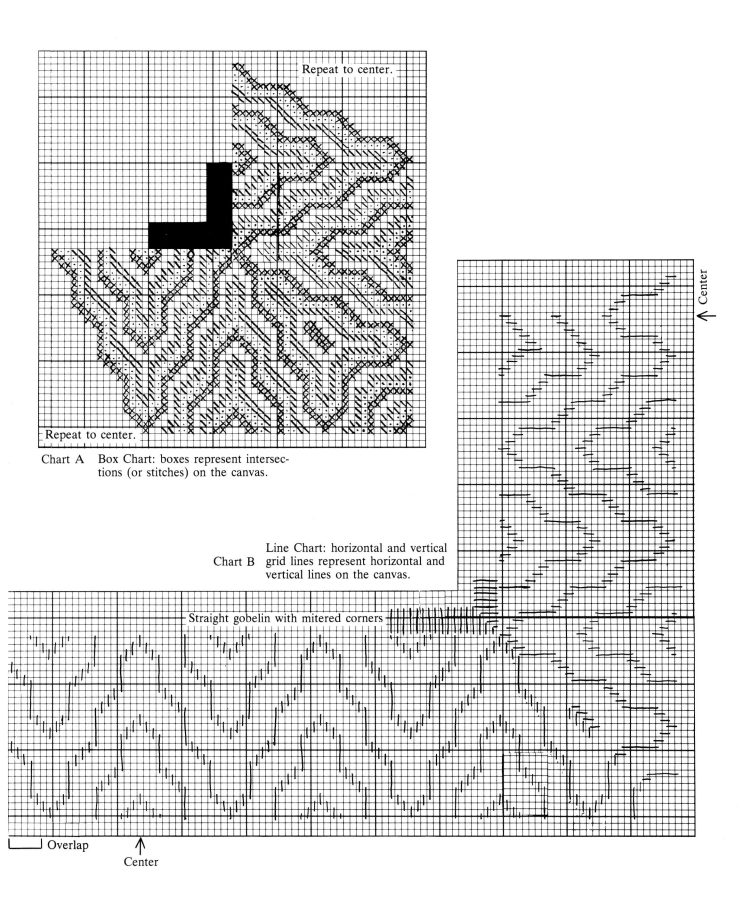

Repeat to center.

Chart A   Box Chart: boxes represent intersections (or stitches) on the canvas.

Repeat to center.

Chart B   Line Chart: horizontal and vertical
grid lines represent horizontal and
vertical lines on the canvas.

← Center

Straight gobelin with mitered corners

⌐ Overlap

↑
Center

BORDER #3

Black & White Shells (page 90) is the central design shown with this border pattern. The colors used with that design are black, medium gray, light gray, and white. Should a border be needed in different colors, these could easily be changed to dark, medium, and light shades of any color with cream or white as the fourth shade.

Color Code (Paterna):
- ◉ black (050)
- ⊠ medium gray (162)
- ◹ light gray (166)
- □ white (012)

Chart A

Box Chart: boxes represent intersections (or stitches) on the canvas.

Instructions:

Follow the general instructions for Bargello Borders, page 115.

Use 3-ply yarn.

If the central design is not perfectly square, the geometric pattern may be different along vertical and horizontal sides of the border.

Chart B

Line Chart: horizontal and vertical grid lines represent horizontal and vertical lines on the canvas.

Work pattern in darkest shade of color code.

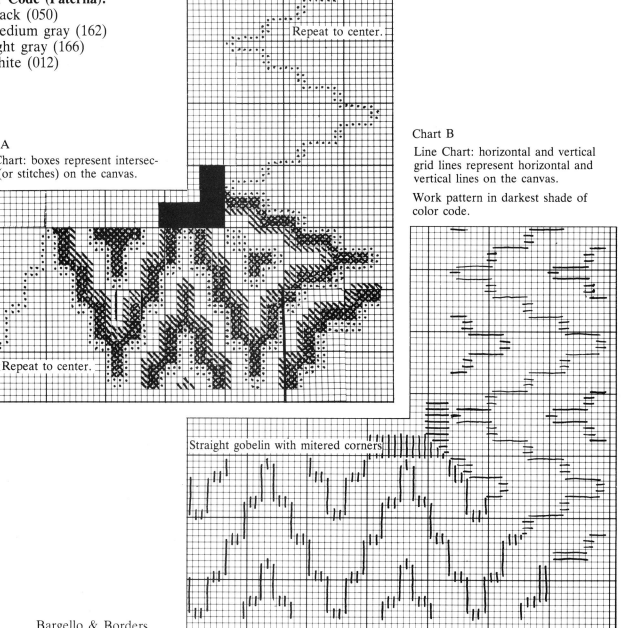

Repeat to center.

Repeat to center.

Straight gobelin with mitered corners

Suppliers

All of the supplies suggested in *Classics for Needlepoint* are widely available in needlework shops. Should you have difficulty locating supplies in your area, however, contact the following companies for a list of retail outlets near you.

CANVAS
Zweigart canvas
Silver Needle of Ohio
Post Office Box 8740
Canton, Ohio 44711

Brown mono #13 canvas
Elsa Williams
Needlecraft House
445 Main Street
West Townsend, Massachusetts 01474

YARN
Paternayan Brothers
Sales Division
312 East 95th Street
New York, New York 10023

MARKERS
AD Markers
Chart Pak
1 River Road
Leeds, Massachusetts 01053

Nepo® Markers
Sanford Corporation
Consumer Service Division
Bellwood, Illinois 60104

Metric Chart

INCHES	CM	INCHES	CM
⅛	3mm	19	48.5
¼	6mm	20	51
⅜	1	21	53.5
½	1.3	22	56
⅝	1.5	23	58.5
¾	2	24	61
⅞	2.2	25	63.5
1	2.5	26	66
1¼	3.2	27	68.5
1½	3.8	28	71
1¾	4.5	29	73.5
2	5	30	76
2½	6.3	31	78.5
3	7.5	32	81.5
3½	9	33	84
4	10	34	86.5
4½	11.5	35	89
5	12.5	36	91.5
5½	14	37	94
6	15	38	96.5
7	18	39	99
8	20.5	40	102
9	23	41	104
10	25.5	42	107
11	28	43	109
12	30.5	44	112
13	33	45	115
14	35.5	46	117
15	38	47	120
16	40.5	48	122
17	43	49	125
18	46	50	127

Index